Your Microcosm
The astrological planets

Marina Kuhn

www.astrologymarina.com

Copyright © 2015 Marina Kuhn

All rights reserved.

ISBN: **1514711311**
ISBN-13: **978-1514711316**

THANK YOU…

To my family for their encouragement,
to those who read my blog for supporting me,
and to Robin for helping me with the editing.
Lastly, thank *you* for reading this book.
I hope you can find a piece of truth in it that will make you feel
less alone in what you're experiencing externally or internally.

CONTENTS

We are microcosms	3
The psychological alphabet of the Universe	8
Exploring your inner cosmos	19
Sun	29
Sun in the Signs	39
Sun in the Houses	42
Moon	47
Moon in the Signs	54
Moon in the Houses	57
Mercury	60
Mercury in the Signs	67
Mercury in the Houses	70
Venus	73
Venus in the Signs	80
Venus in the Houses	83
Mars	86
Mars in the Signs	91
Mars in the Houses	94

Jupiter	97
Jupiter in the Houses	105
Saturn	108
Saturn in the Houses	119
Uranus	123
Uranus in the Houses	130
Neptune	133
Neptune in the Houses	140
Pluto	144
Pluto in the Houses	153
Epilogue	157

"It does not matter what kind of flower you are.
What matters is flowering."

Osho

WE ARE MICROCOSMS

*"Astrology is the study of the anatomy
and psychology of God."*
Manly Hall

When you first meet someone, they're just another person. One out of billions of strangers on this planet. Not to mention the countless generations that have come before us or that are to come after us. But soon you will realize that this particular stranger is just as complex a human being as you are – that they have years of memories, decisions, experiences, triumphs and fails leading up to their first meeting with you. They probably have that random childhood memory about the wrapping paper of their favorite popsicle, the hurtful comment that was ingrained into their brains in high school and their own unique mental representation of the word "carpet". The more you get to know someone, the more you realize that, truly, they're their own little universe.

The universe is kind of like a Russian doll – containing itself again and again in yet smaller forms. Our solar system is but an atom of the universe. The cells in our bodies, each and every single one of them, contain all information about us. A cell is like a microcosm of a body. Then can we be a microcosm of the solar system? In astrology (*astro logos, to make sense of the stars*) we believe that the planetary alignments within the solar system at the time and place of someone's birth describe that individual's personality and life. People would consequently be the embodiment of a certain moment in space-time.

Your Microcosm

Every child is born into a specific arrangement of celestial bodies and each of them represents an archetypal principle. The solar system at the moment of a child's first breath, with all its energetic interplays and potentials, imprints itself onto the mind of the newborn baby. So, what astrology basically says is that we are a sort of extension of the universe, a representation of it in human form.

There are probably many layers inherent in this microcosm-macrocosm structure that are smaller than the cells in our bodies and larger than our universe that we are not even aware of. There seems to be an underlying pattern that connects everything and makes everything alike, no matter at what scale. That's what the ancient alchemical principle "As above, so below" is about. Although light, heat and electromagnetic rays as well as gravitational pulls reach us from the planets of the solar system, I like to think that it's not the actual celestial bodies that have this astrological influence on us. Rather, they're just yet another representation of the patterns and structures inherent in this universe that organize everything. It's not Venus that affects us by sending down magical waves; Venus is an embodiment and representation of that effect that exerts itself on the whole cosmos. Our solar system is one of many microcosms inherent in this Russian doll universe, so it's just a representation of something even bigger – just like the cells in our bodies represent the genetics of our whole body.

Alan Watts said that "as the ocean 'waves', the universe 'peoples'". A wave is a thing in itself yet completely inseparable from the entirety of the ocean. Every soul is like a stream born from a soul ocean. It is impossible for the human mind to fully conceptualize of the fact that there is nothing but the universe, that there is nothing outside of it. Our reality is one of relativity, where we can only define things in relation to other things. I am me, because I am not you – or this rock or this tree. This building is tall because the one next to it is small. But there is nothing outside of the universe (*universum, all encompassing*) so there's nothing to compare it to and define it through. We live in a world of cause and effect. But there is no cause of the universe, because if it is the only thing in existence, nothing outside of itself could have caused it. It just is. And it is all that there is. Some people call this all-encompassing presence inherent in all life God. In "The Book: The Taboo against knowing who you are", Watts writes: "God also likes to play hide-and-seek, but because there is nothing outside God, he has no one but himself to play with. But he gets over this difficulty by pretending that he is not himself. This is his way of hiding from himself. He pretends that he is you and I and all the people in the world, all the animals, all the plants, all the rocks, and all the stars."

Everything in existence would then merely be a thought within an infinite consciousness. The universe is then mental rather than physical. We are just the product of a momentary thought in the mind of god or the universe. Since the universe is mental, since it is *the mind*, the consciousness out of which everything arises, astrology is a way of studying the psychology of the universe, becoming aware of and analyzing the mind that has thought us into existence. We are of course but a tiny fraction of the mental processes of the universe so we will never be able to fully grasp and understand the enormity of it.

Just like a mole rat would never understand the concept of vision and just like we can never fully mentally grasp what five dimensions would look like (sure, a fourth dimension could be seen as adding time to the three-dimensional space, but then what?) there is no point in getting caught up in trying to conceptualize of something that is outside of human understanding. Some people make "spiritual enlightenment" their goal, to transcend their personal boundaries, become one with the whole cosmos, and take in the perspective of god consciousness. Personally, I have learned to fall in love with this game, with being a unique expression of universal patterns and archetypes, seeing them in myself and in others. We would not be human if it had not been our intention in the first place.

The cosmos individualized itself as people purposely. The planets are constantly cycling around the sun on their own orbit, forming unique patterns, depending on their mathematical relationships to each other. What a birth chart or a horoscope of a person is, is a snapshot of the constellations of the celestial bodies at the time and in relationship to the place on earth they were born. If you take a snapshot of every moment in the universe, it creates a continuum, and you could cut out individual slices and they would be the birth chart of a person. That birth chart is a moment in space-time and it represent the person – their personality, their life potentials, their celestial, psychological imprints. We are snapshots of our solar system. We are a conscious expression of a moment in space-time, we are the cosmos individualized as a person.

What this says about the meaning of life or our individual purpose is that this is an opportunity for the universe, for God, to explore itself, to become conscious of itself. To actively experience the archetypes, play around with them and become able to grasp them. Every birth chart is a new combination of archetypes, a new possibility for the universe to get to know itself – because nothing is outside of it, it has to define itself by looking inside itself.

A person's iris is as unique as a fingerprint. The galaxy-like patterns and the star-like specks make it look like a little universe. We all know the phrase "the eyes are the window to the soul" but have you ever studied someone's iris and felt that their soul was really just a snapshot of the cosmos?

You will soon realize that this particular stranger is not a universe. They are *the* universe. The same one as you. In yet another disguise.

THE PSYCHOLOGICAL ALPHABET OF THE UNIVERSE

"In one drop of water are found all the secrets of all the oceans; in one aspect of You are found all the aspects of existence."
Khalil Gibran

I now want to get deeper into the specifics of the underlying patterns and structures of *the mind*. Albert Einstein said that "no problem can be solved from the same level of consciousness that created it" and if the universe (God) created all these formulas, that means the parts of the astrological chart and their interplays, we won't ever be able to fully understand them. Instead of pointing out what Mercury means, we can associate it with "mind", "intellect", "communication" - all of the above *are related to* Mercury, but none of them *are* Mercury.

The associations are not the archetype. The archetypes will, in their essence, stay forever untouchable to the human mind, because we did not create them, we are created from them. We are expressions of those archetypes, so our consciousness is not able to grasp them. That is, of course, the problem with trying to prove astrology – we can't ever do it. Nor can we disprove it. It would be like a Sim becoming conscious of the fact that it is in a computer game and then trying to figure out how the game The Sims has been programmed (actually, scientists are now analyzing the theory that the universe is a computer simulation).

We can simply observe and find things to associate with the archetypes – which is the astrological alphabet of the zodiac signs, planets and houses. When you first get into astrology, you might only care about the zodiac signs, but the more you study astrological charts, the more you realize that the planets are the protagonists of the chart and that the signs and houses form a kind of backdrop to them. The planets are the parts of our psyche. They have been turned into gods and goddesses in mythologies all over the globe, since the beginning of the human race. You can see the same stories coming up in cultures all around the world. That is what an archetype is, by the way: an image or story that exists in the minds of people independent of cultural, ethnic and geographical background – independent of time and space. These are the universals of the experience of life. Fairytale-, movie- and book characters such as the witch, the hero, the sidekick, the villain, the rebel without a cause, plot devices such as the initiation, the point of no return, the grand finale and the return home – all these universals that make up the narrative of all cultures across the globe and throughout human history.

Carl Jung has come up with the theory of the collective unconscious, which says that we, each of us, do not have a collective unconscious mind but are in fact embedded in it, like water that is always surrounding us, and as humanity develops, we collectively add to this mind and we all have more or less conscious access to it.

At the smallest scale, there is no such thing as "matter", everything is energy. That energy that animates all of life has been called *chi* in the Chinese tradition and *prana* in India, and there are many more names for this vital energy that has been categorized into yin and yang (the light and dark, feminine and masculine), the four temperaments melancholic, phlegmatic, sanguine and choleric and the associated bodily fluids or humours blood, yellow bile, black bile and phlegm, which were believed to have to be in balance in order to provide physical and mental health. There have been distinctions into elements in different cultures, both in the east and the west – the striking similarity is that people have always seen a kind of system which divides the basic energy into different types of expression. In astrology, there are the four elements of fire, earth, air and water as well as the three qualities of cardinal, fixed and mutable.

>**Fire:** Energetic, motivational, inspirational
>
>**Earth:** Pragmatic, realistic, reliable
>
>**Air:** Intellectual, logic, sociable
>
>**Water:** Emotional, intuitive, empathetic
>
>**Cardinal:** Direct, assertive, initiates and begins
>
>**Fixed:** Slow, steady, finishes and pulls through
>
>**Mutable:** Adaptable, scattered, shares and learns

Each sign in the Zodiac Wheel is a combination of one element and one quality and is associated with one of the planets and houses.

Your Microcosm

1. Aries, cardinal fire, Mars, 1st House
2. Taurus, fixed earth, Venus, 2nd House
3. Gemini, mutable air, Mercury, 3rd House
4. Cancer, cardinal water, Moon, 4th House
5. Leo, fixed fire, Sun, 5th House
6. Virgo, mutable earth, Mercury, 6th House
7. Libra, cardinal air, Venus, 7th House
8. Scorpio, fixed water, Pluto, 8th House
9. Sagittarius, mutable fire, Jupiter, 9th House
10. Capricorn, cardinal earth, Saturn, 10th House
11. Aquarius, fixed air, Uranus, 11th House
12. Pisces, mutable water, Neptune, 12th House

These are the twelve letters of the Astrological Alphabet – although the signs, planets and houses of each respective letter mean slightly different things, they represent a common archetypal theme. This is what the different components of the astrological letters stand for:

> **Planets:** parts of our psyche, the gods and goddesses that incarnate and act through us, archetypal expressions of universal energy
>
> **Signs:** a sort of stained glass window in front of the planets, coloring the expression of them, giving them

unique qualities and traits and influencing the way their energetic principle is expressed

Houses: areas of experience, parts of our lives and selves in which the planetary energies, colored by the traits of the zodiac signs, are expressed in

An analogy that I really like is seeing the planets as actors, who take on the roles or costumes of the signs they're in and play on the stages indicated by the houses they're in. By exploring the positions of the planets in the signs and houses, you will achieve a great understanding of yourself – which is probably my personal favorite part of astrology. These are just a few of the things you can learn;

> **Sun**: Why do I act and express myself the way I do?
> **Moon**: Why do I react and feel the way I do?
> **Mercury**: Why do I think and communicate the way I do?
> **Venus**: Why do I express affection the way I do?
> **Mars**: Why do I express anger and passion the way I do?
> **Jupiter**: Where do I feel most confident and where do I push my luck?
> **Saturn**: Where do I feel most anxious and where do I need to realize authority?
> **Uranus**: Where do I rebel and innovate?
> **Neptune**: Where do I lose touch with reality and escape it?
> **Pluto**: Where do I feel most powerless and need to let go of ego to transform?

Through an easy keyword system, one can get a general idea of what each placement of a planet in a sign and house means. Simply fill in the blanks to form a sentence describing your birth chart placements;

I express my _____ (planet) in a _____ (sign) way and it is primarily focused at _____ (house).

Sun: identity
Moon: emotions
Mercury: thoughts
Venus: charm and affection
Mars: assertion and passion
Jupiter: wisdom and beliefs
Saturn: authority or fear
Uranus: rebellion and innovation
Neptune: imagination and escapism
Pluto: power and powerlessness

Cancer: sensitive and nurturing
Leo: dramatic and generous
Virgo: productive and serving
Libra: fair and charming
Scorpio: intense and deep
Sagittarius: idealistic and exaggerated
Capricorn: responsible and ambitious
Aquarius: individualistic and eccentric
Pisces: passive and allowing

Aries: direct and assertive
Taurus: slow and sensual
Gemini: quick and intellectual

1st House: my identity
2nd House: my self-worth and possessions

3rd House: the way I express my ideas and communicate
4th House: my family and home life, my privacy
5th House: my creativity, talents and hobbies
6th House: my routine and health
7th House: other people and relationships
8th House: my secrets and personal transformations
9th House: my worldview and education
10th House: my image in the public and my career
11th House: my network and aspirations
12th House: my unconscious and behind-the-scenes

To get a first idea and image of your chart, you can write out a sentence of each of your placements on a sheet of paper.

Generally speaking, the sun is our point of consciousness and the further away a planet is from the sun - all the way from Mercury to Pluto - the more unconscious and the more collective their respective principle is.
The farther away from the sun, the bigger the orbit and the longer the path around the sun. That is why the outer planets are also known as generational planets, since they stay in one sign for many years and color generations more so than individuals – contrary to the sun, which changes signs every month, or the moon, which changes signs every 2,5 days! This is why, in this book, there will be descriptions of all planets in the houses, but only the inner, personal planets in the signs of the zodiac! I think a clearer description and distinction of signs and houses would be appropriate here:

Signs: Division of the ecliptic (the plane on which all planets except for Pluto, reside and orbit) into 12 equal parts. The signs are, in western tropical astrology, divisions of the sky and not the actual constellations.

Houses: Depend on the diurnal (daily) motion of the earth, that means the earth spinning around its own axis. As the earth spins around itself once a day, all planets pass through all twelve houses within that day. This makes houses more individual, since they change every few hours – it shows their placement relative to the horizon and other points in the sky that change throughout the day.

There are more factors that play into the life and personality of a person other than the astrological ones – gender identity, ethnicity, cultural, societal, historic and geographical background and so on. Yet these astrological archetypes are completely universal and independent of these factors – archetypes conquer barriers set by time or space. My twin sister and I were born a mere minute apart through c-section, so we pretty much share a birth chart. This has been a perfect opportunity for me to explore and analyze the things that are "set in stone" in a birth chart and those that are individual and independent of the horoscope. By comparing myself and my life to that of my sister, I have come to realize that horoscopes show distinct potentials but no specific outcomes. The two of us always joke about how talking to each other is like becoming more conscious of yourself, like conversing with yourself, your own subconscious. Our conversations always accelerate self-awareness and personal growth.

The astrological birth chart is all about potential – about the easiest and most natural flow of energy. You can let yourself be dragged downstream and have all the worst possibilities indicated in your chart come true, or, with self-awareness and the willingness to grow, make great use of your potentials. As the level of consciousness rises, the level of free will rises. As we free ourselves from subconscious dictations, we free ourselves from dictations of "destiny".

The letters of the astrological alphabet, the twelve zodiac signs, the twelve houses and the ten planets, are what structure the whole universe but also each individual. A random person like you, living somewhere on this planet, for a period of time that won't even add up to a mere blink of an eye in the life of the universe, might feel very small. We might feel like the gods are without but they're equally within. You can call upon the gods, which is really just to make the unconscious conscious. The planetary archetypes are energetic patterns stored in the collective unconscious that are individualized in the personal unconscious, depending on the unique placement of that planet in someone's birth chart. If Venus is in Taurus in your chart, for example, you will channel the collective energetic pattern of affection in a sensual way. All letters of the astrological language are just specific energies or vibrations that we as humans personify. We live in a quantum universe where everything is energy. A table is made up of the same energy as the feeling of love, the thought "I like pudding" or a tree – the energy just vibrates at different frequencies to create these "things". Reality is not so much a hallucination, though, as it is a projection. The universal mind, that is split up into individual consciousnesses, is the projector. If your chart then shows that you are a pessimistic person who sees limitations everywhere, this makes you a certain type of projector that will project those things into their reality. That is how I see the interrelatedness of the personality and the life experience being shown in the birth chart. Personality creates personal reality. You have a limited view on life, which will make your life be limited, which will reassure you of your belief that life is limited and so on. We create our reality according to what we believe about it. A belief is a thought we have thought enough to make it unconscious and automatic, we think it without realizing and it orders our reality accordingly without us realizing.

If we are, for example, born into a family that keeps on telling us "Money doesn't grow on trees, you only earn it through hard work!", and we internalize those beliefs, we will keep on looking for money in places where it is hard to get, we will conclude that earning money is tough, which will strengthen the belief "money is earned only through suffering" and it is a vicious downwards spiral, leading us deeper into a financial struggle.

Once we are aware of the beliefs we hold and the unconscious patterns that control us and our lives, we can work to exalt them – to make the best possible use of those potentials. For example, the belief about hard-earned money might come from Saturn in the 2nd house. That same placement, however, also indicates that money is taken seriously and dealt with responsibly. So you could change the belief "earning money is hard" into "I take full responsibility of my finances and handle them effectively". That is why there is no such thing as an inherently bad or inherently good placement in astrology. Challenging configurations urge us to grow and easy configurations might keep us stuck in the same behavior that has always seemed to work – until it doesn't.

Our whole reality is shaped by our beliefs because they are our most automatic and unconscious thoughts. We don't even know what our beliefs are until we actively explore them.

In the system of the Astrological Alphabet, we are stories written across the cosmos. We are daydreams of the universal psyche. When we realize we are daydreaming, we can change that dream through our awareness.

EXPLORING YOUR INNER COSMOS

"There's as many atoms in a single molecule of your DNA as there are stars in the typical galaxy. We are each of us, a little universe."
Neil deGrasse Tyson

The pitfalls and benefits of studying astrology

I think I've gotten into astrology the way most people do: reading about "my sign" and going "That's so me! Tell me more about myself!" At first, discovering your zodiac sign traits can feel like a big relief, an identity to hold on to. *Especially* in your teenage years, when we all struggle to carve out an identity for ourselves. It's so satisfying to go "I'm such a typical Sagittarius." Whenever someone asks us to talk about ourselves, we now have all these traits associated with our sign to list: "Well, you know, I'm a real optimist and idealist. I'm an adventurer at heart and can be quite restless." I think over identifying with your sign is very dangerous, though. You will realize that you will outgrow that description more and more – that you are much more complex than this very simple archetype. If, even then, you still try to hold onto your sun sign as a means of having a sense of identity, you will start becoming a caricature of yourself. No one will ever be a "typical Sagittarius", because there is so much more to us than this one sign – we're a unique combination of all the signs. Trying to play out your birth chart is not being yourself. Exaggerating all the traits associated with your placements is not authenticity. Don't worry about *becoming* your chart, because you can't not be it.

We can't experience or act out any parts of our chart in isolation – my Sagittarius sun in the 12th house will manifest differently from that of someone else, because it's delicately interwoven with the unique rest of my chart. That is why even personal experience will not make you understand how somebody else truly feels about that same placement in their own chart. Everyone has the same parts in their chart – just in different combinations. That's why, when you say "I hate Virgos!" – guess what – you're just hating that part within yourself. We are all mirrors to each other. We are the universe becoming conscious of itself, remembering itself after playing hide-and-seek, seeing its own face in every person they meet along the path. I love this sense of connection that comes from realizing we're all made up of the same parts, experiencing similar things.

The best we can do is simply living our own truth. It is good to know that the whole universe conspired to make us exactly who we are and that the best we can contribute is our authenticity. Maybe the reason nothing fascinates us as much as the rawness and vulnerability of authenticity does and that everyone is looking for "the truth" is because – that's what God is. I invite you to commit yourself to truth and honesty, to meet life and people with your arms spread wide open, ready to express the raw and unedited version of yourself. It is hard, it is probably the hardest thing we will ever do, but that is why it is the most important thing. Authenticity is magnetic and contagious. Nothing is as brave as vulnerability and the act of refusing to accept anything but the truth.

Although we have to avoid the trap of over-identifying with our charts or justifying awful behavior with it, studying your horoscope is an amazing tool of self awareness.

As teenagers, especially, we dislike ourselves, because we get angry and frustrated with ourselves - we don't understand why we act the way we do, why we feel the way we do. We don't know why certain things affect us and have the impact on us that they do. It seems like these random unpredictable things and like we fail for no reason. We are highly unaware of what makes us special and unique and where our talents and capabilities lie.

I think it was Thich Nhat Hanh who said that understanding is love. When you truly understand someone, where they are coming from, you can't help but love them. If your childhood bully revealed the hurt he experienced from his father neglecting him, if you really put yourself in his position, you wouldn't hate him.

If you are so aware of why you are the way you are, where those psychological patterns come from and how they are expressed within you, you can't help but understand, accept and finally learn to love yourself. And that's how it works with looking at the charts of other people as well.

Another common trap of astrology was described by Liz Greene, who said that a lot of astrologers and students of astrology use the astrological language as a defense mechanism, of which I am completely guilty myself.

Astrology allows you to express complicated, emotional and spiritual concepts in a symbolic language.
I love talking to people with a knowledge of astrology, because it allows me to communicate my innermost being without having to go on an awkward emotional ramble. Instead of saying "I've not been very successful with building long-lasting, close friendships in the past" I will just tell them that I have a strong 11th house Pluto. Instead of saying "Anger makes me cry and crying makes me angry and I have the most uncontrollable, extreme outbursts of emotions" I can just say "I have a Moon Mars conjunction in the 8th house."
And they will know and I won't have to explain myself and it won't feel as weird and personal because using the symbolic language of astrology gives you more distance to the topic, like you are taking a step back from the emotional aspect and looking at it very scientifically.

When chatting with new-found friends who are astrology students too, we usually lay out our whole psyche and life story within that first conversation – we simply send each other a picture of our birth charts and then talk about it a bit. This might seem quite casual but we usually already know each other quite intimately at this point. That is why talking to people who don't know a lot or anything at all about astrology can be frustrating to me; they aren't very self-aware at all and I have to keep myself from explaining their own lives to them and being the preachy Sagittarius that I am.
I have found myself using this defense mechanism a lot, even with people who don't have a clue about astrology. It's just become my excuse to not open up and not talk

about things on an emotional level, from a vulnerable place. Make sure to be aware of whether you are using astrology to understand yourself and grow or whether you are using it to hide behind a persona, justify your weaknesses and escape emotional vulnerability.

Is astrology science or religion?

Our senses are selective. You can see less than 1% of the electromagnetic spectrum and hear less than 1% of the acoustic spectrum. Some animals can't see rainbows because they don't have the receptors needed. So you don't just see a rainbow, you create it. Everything you experience with your senses sight, touch, smell, taste, sound does not exist on itself - you create it in your mind. Everything is just electromagnetic waves until your body translates it into a sound, a sight etc. That's why you say "If a tree falls down in a forest and nobody is there to hear it, it makes no sound."
The radio waves of all broadcasting stations are surrounding you at this very moment, but you can only hear them if you switch the radio on to a specific channel and it "translates" them. Because your brain is not capable of doing that.
There are energies you are not aware of and that you cannot translate and therefore experience but this does not mean that they do not exist. Just because gravity was not discovered or scientifically proven yet, does not mean it did not exist and did not have an impact on life on earth.

Astrology is not considered a science (anymore). But what

is science and what is not is only based on the human ability to measure it by themselves or with the help of instruments – which is a very restricting view on reality.

Once you have studied astrology and your personal chart for a certain amount of time, you will realize that there are no deities and powers outside of you. All these mythological gods and goddesses are mere symbols and personifications of the energies within the whole universe. Astrology is then not religious but spiritual.

When God created humans in his image, what they were saying is – God (the universe) is an infinite consciousness with nothing outside of it – so it had to create within itself – God created humans in his imagination.

Da Vinci was the one who had popularly reconnected the dots and saw the spiritual meaning and zodiacal symbolism in the Bible (as described, for example, in Dan Brown's *The Da Vinci Code*). In his painting of the last supper, Jesus represents the sun in the center while the surrounding twelve disciples of Christ are separated into four groups of three – representing the seasons and the zodiac signs. The last supper was a painting of the path of the sun along the zodiac throughout the year.

In the painting *The Creation of Adam* by Michelangelo, which shows God touching the finger of the first human created, God is painted within a brain. Since autopsy was illegal back then, no one understood the allusion towards God existing in the mind. One of the things about the nature of the universe is that opposites complement each other – God exists in our minds, because we exist in God's mind.

That is the core of pretty much all world religions that has been misunderstood or warped in meaning today. Most religions teach unity and love and it's only the details surrounding that separate them.

Destiny and free will

Carl Jung once said that "Until you make the unconscious conscious, it will direct your life and you will call it fate". We are born with all these potentials indicated in our birth chart, but we are mostly unaware of them. Without the tool of astrology, it could take a lifetime to become aware of our internal psychological structures that drive and control us. As long as we are unconscious of them, they will unknowingly control us and our lives. However, through studying your own horoscope, you bring your psychological imprints into the light of consciousness. This is when they lose control over you. This is sort of like walking a route that is very familiar to you, that makes you switch on autopilot and then suddenly realizing you have been unconscious the whole time, staring into empty space and just going where you are naturally pulled to. It is then that you regain free will to choose whether you want to stay on that path or go somewhere completely different.

In the previous chapter I explained how we adopted beliefs about us and our lives that now run our reality. All that reality is, is perception. My sister actually pointed out to me that the German word for perception, *Wahrnehmung*, can literally be translated into "true-taking". It is what we take as true, and that is why it is true to us. Reality is BS – Belief systems. Beliefs aren't objective truths but they are our personal reality.

The gods are not outside of us, controlling us – they are in our own unconscious. If we become conscious of them, we regain their powers. The mere awareness of the patterning psychological energies at work will move the gods outside of you, inside of you. Everything in the unconscious is automatic, it has effect on us without our conscious awareness. If we become conscious of the gods in the collective unconscious, we will become them – through our conscious access to these energies.

Your birth chart shows your karmic makeup as well as your conditions in early life, but as you grow up, those gods outside of you are realized to be inside. You have endless possibilities of working with your chart. Fate lies in psychic structures. Once they are changed, our fate changes.

The universe is constantly communicating with us through synchronistic events. It has been said that coincidences are spiritual puns or God's way of staying anonymous, that it is the universe winking at you. Your dreams at night is your own subconscious communicating with you through symbols. You too can communicate with the universe and your own subconscious through symbols – by taking actions with symbolic meaning, also called rituals. I am not taking about demonic séances here, it can be something small like throwing out all the stuff you don't need any more, standing in front of the dumpster and throwing away your trash with full awareness of the symbolic meaning of this event – you are making room for new experiences, you are ending an old way of living or a former phase in your life.

We perform rituals every day, like getting ready in the morning and following the routine of showering, brushing our teeth and so on. Become more aware of the underlying meaning of everything happening to you and everything you do and your life will regain the magic as if seen through the eyes of a fascinated child. There is magic and meaning everywhere, the whole cosmos is ruled by archetypal, planetary gods and goddesses and you always have access to these energies.

If you want to remember your dreams, simply set the intention. Some might want to make a sort of ritual where they write something down or speak a phrase but just consciously setting the intention "I want to remember my dream" before you close your eyes and go to sleep is enough. When you create a huge ritual surrounding this, you might want it to work so badly and build so much resistance against it not working that you fail.

Have pen and paper ready next to your bed so that in the moments of waking up, still being half caught-up in your dream, you are reminded to hold onto that dream and start writing down as many details as possible. There's no real point in looking up dream interpretations online because only you can really know what it means - a dream is your own subconscious communicating with you through symbols. Write down what you think you were trying to convey to yourself. If you get better at remembering dreams, you can ask to get answers to specific questions through dreams.

This is a good way to become more conscious of what is unconscious, to communicate with our innermost being, to move the gods within and take control of where we are going, to direct our own destiny through our free will.

SUN

"I want to exist from my own force, like the sun, which gives light and does not suck light."
Carl Jung

The sun is a giant ball of fire glowing brightly in the center of our solar system while all the other celestial bodies are revolving around it. Its light and warmth makes life on earth possible, it gives structure to the bodies floating around in space, it serves as a center. The sun is the center of the solar system, and since we are the expression of the solar system at a certain point in space and time, the sun in our astrological chart is *our center*. A word often associated with the astrological sun is "ego". Ego means our sense of being separate from everything else, having a unique identity. The sun is our *self-consciousness*, as in our awareness that we are an individual, an independent person.

The symbol of the sun is the circle of the self with the point of consciousness in the middle. The circle symbolizes the infinite whole, no beginning and no end, the all-encompassing presence within all that is. The dot in the middle of the circle represents that spark of awareness and consciousness within the whole. It stands for individuation – it is the individual awareness focused within the all.

People will literally gravitate towards someone with a strong sun. They are generous, loving and emit the same level of light and warmth as the sun. This is the archetype of the savior – it was the first celestial body to be worshipped, because it allowed the crops to grow and saved us from the dangers of the dark night. Every morning, the light triumphs over the night and saves us. Holy figures such as Jesus are portrayed with a halo, which looks like the sun at the back of their head – these are the sun deities, the savior archetypes.

Without the sun, there would be no light or warmth on this earth. Without the sun in our chart, there would be no spark of life and no light of consciousness. The sun thinks it's the center of the whole universe. It makes us think that we are the protagonist of the story, that others are just minor characters who support the hero or heroine (that is us). If we were constantly aware of the fact that everyone has as complex a mind and life as we do, life would be overwhelming and we would probably be very passive, timid and lifeless.

The sun is essential, because it is the planet that puts us on the driver's seat of life, it's what makes us take action and participate in life. A weak or debilitated sun can make one have ego-issues, making one feel like a mere supporting character, a sidekick rather than a hero, like being in the passenger seat of life.

The sun describes what we identify ourselves as and our need for that to be seen, to have an impact as an individual, to exert our will. It's the creative energy that wants to draw the colors of their unique personality across the canvas of this world – our need to express ourselves and leave our footprints on this planet. It is our personal power, our impact as a person, our sense of existing, taking in space. The sun is huge so it takes in a great amount of space, and the sun in your chart will show how much personal space you feel comfortable taking in or you feel you deserve taking in.

The sun determines whether and how you take action, exert your will and express your unique identity. It makes you feel like you are important and have an impact, like there is no one just like you, like you are special and deserve your place in this universe, as if you were specifically created to be here, be who you are and do what you do.

A weak sun will make you feel like you can't or don't want to take in space. It makes you quiet and small. When you talk and notice that everyone's attention is focused on you, you will panic, thinking "Am I worthy of taking up their time by having them listen to what I am saying? I should hurry and end my sentence so I don't waste people's' time, I am unimportant and what I say is unimportant, too". The sun is tied to our self-worth; what we feel we are worthy of, or not. Someone with a strong sun will have a healthy ego, naturally demanding attention, assuming the role of the entertainer and liking it. This can, of course, be exaggerated, too, making someone constantly thirsty for attention, needing to be seen and heard by everyone, pushing themselves onto others, fishing for compliments.

There is this saying that insecurities are loud and

confidence is silent. A person who is sure of themselves doesn't feel the need to have others tell them that they're worthy (although it's still nice) and they don't feel the need to defend criticism, because they simply know who they are and who they are not.

The sun is also associated with pride. We can only be proud of things that we think are extraordinary, unlike everything else, rare and special. The sun makes us feel like we are special, one of a kind. It separates us from others, making us think that we are not everything else – so it really is the first step of the universe splitting itself up into different consciousnesses, individualizing itself. Every other planet merely adds to and supports this sense of ego – this haughty attitude that we are special and unique and that we're the only ones going through or experiencing the things associated with the other planets the same way others do. Every other planet quite literally merely revolves around the center that is the sun.

The Sun is our self-concept. The sign it is in indicates how we consciously act and express our individuality. This luminary is the means of our identification. The sun in our chart says "I am!". Next to the gender, race or social role we identify with, the sun sign shows the archetype we identify with the most. Sun in Sagittarius might say "I am a teacher!" That's why most people relate so much to their sun sign and feel it is the major part of their personality, it is what they primarily identify as. The sun is exalted in Aries. Here it says "I am a hero!" Someone with their sun in Aries really feels they are the leading role. They initiate and are action-oriented but also a bit egoistic.

The sun shines majestically in the center of our solar system, on its celestial throne – royal and regal. It naturally demands attention and whenever it shows itself after a dark night or a cold winter, it is considered a blessing, an honor. When it gets to a point where we personally feel like our presence is a blessing or an honor, it can tip over in arrogance. Since the sun is tied to everything about us we feel is important, deserves recognition and to be in the spotlight – if it takes up our whole being, we can develop hubris, a feeling of being divine, all-mighty and omniscient.

As I mentioned before, the sun was the first celestial body to be exalted into divinity, related with deities or gods. In our individual lives, the first apparent "gods" we come across are our parents.

The sun in our birth chart stands for the father, his influence on us and our perception of him. This is the archetype of the hero, the savior, the king – what we perceive our father as in early life. All-mighty, generous father. Even if he was abusive, he was a god to us. And if he didn't treat us well, we concluded we must have deserved it. How can a god possibly be wrong? This is how low self-esteem develops. We believe that the way our parents treat us is absolutely legitimate. A weak or challenged sun shows a weak or challenging father that limited the development of our sense of self-worth and confidence. Often, an absent or passive father raises (or fails to raise) shy and timid children who believe they aren't worthy of any attention. Then there's also those children who desperately seek approval and try to win over the love of daddy in another person who subconsciously reminds them of their father – the infamous Oedipus complex or "Daddy issues" in girls.

The sign that the sun is in shows what is important to us but not necessarily what we actually embody. With more confidence and willpower, we are more likely to pursue the things important to us. So, the stronger the sun (our confidence and heroism), the more we identify with our sun sign traits. Since the sun is connected to the father and how we perceive him, he is also the reason these sun sign traits become so important to us in the first place. Winning the love of our father meant he recognized what we did well, what was special about us. The traits and characteristics he saw as important became a crucial measurement of our personal self-worth. Therefore, this becomes important to us. Someone with a Virgo Sun might have perceived their father as praising them and giving them attention the most when they were working, dutifully fulfilling their tasks, doing homework, cleaning their room, and so on. Virgo Suns are said to be productive and organized, but those who feel disempowered and small might think "I am never going to be in control of this chaos anyway." Only those who trust their capabilities pursue what is important to them and feed their sense of self-worth, which then breeds even more courage for them to go after those things and so on. It's a constant upward or downward spiral.

So the sun is what determines whether you actively exist as an individual or merely passively observe everyone else and just sit at the sideline. Are you the hero or the sidekick of your story? Your probably intuitively know how strong your sun is; how much you let yourself shine, how much personal power and influence you feel you have. The weaker this inner light, the more we fear challenges, because we don't trust in our ability to overcome obstacles and prove ourselves.

In medical astrology, the sun rules our heart. The center of the solar system on the macro-level and the center of the body on the micro-level. The sun in the horoscope is our heart center. Since it shows what is important to us, it also shows what we put our heart into, how and where we dare to be courageous. The French word for heart is cœur, which is etymologically related to core.

Being the ruler of the zodiac sign Leo, the sun is what makes one be "lionhearted" – to be open to challenges and risks, because you are brave and trust your abilities. To be loyal and heroic. The sun impacts our whole vitality, both our physical aliveness but also our will to live on all other levels. It furthermore rules the cardiovascular system, the blood and, obviously, the *solar* plexus.

The solar plexus chakra is an energy center in our body which directly reflects the health of the astrological sun in our horoscope. This chakra is a psychological digestive system, which helps get rid of toxins in both the literal and figurative term. To get rid of toxicity in our life means to honor ourselves to the degree of cutting out anything that doesn't feed into our power and vitality. It also means to have unconstructive criticism be flushed out of our system without having it affect us – it shields us from damages of our confidence and self-worth.

A weak sun or debilitated psychic digestive system leaves one being easily embarrassed, very affected by criticism and in fact, seeing everything as a personal attack and always feeling wrong or bad. When you doubt yourself, when you are nervous and lack confidence, it affects the solar plexus. You have probably had stomach aches before holding a presentation, giving a job interview or anything that made you unsure about your abilities.

Our sense of purpose can be found within this solar energy, and with purpose comes the urge to live, create and express. The weaker our sense of being a special individual with a real effect on their outside world, the more passive, weak and small we are – the less we use our creative resources, because we either don't believe in our talents or we think that what we create is meaningless. Only when we feel like we have something to add to this world do we truly show ourselves with pride and share our creative work – we believe our art is worth being seen. We believe we are worth being seen.

This archetype also rules children, not only because they're so creative and their will to express themselves has not been suppressed yet, but also because they are the biggest signs of the human capacity to create. We can literally create a life. The birth of a new hero. And every year, at their birthday, we celebrate the fact that they were born, that they exist, we celebrate a person simply for the sake of their existence. Every year, on your birthday, the sun returns back to its position in the zodiac of our birth. This is probably a better day for New Year's resolutions than the 1st of January (unless that *is* your birthday, of course), because it is your personal new year – a new cycle of your sun. A new quest of your inner hero(ine).

Whereas the sign the sun is in shows how our inner hero(ine) identifies themselves, the house this luminary is in shows where we want to *shine* and be recognized – it describes the focus of our life. This part of life is illuminated and becomes very important to us, our whole being and energy is put inside this house – we put our heart into this house. Even if we try to pursue other areas of life, we will go back to this one again and again - until we have it figured out and have succeeded there, we can't really focus on anything else.

Every one of us has that inner sun, we all have light and warmth to give to the world. If, however, our sun shines through filters of false personas, stained glass windows of others expectations, its light will be dimmer and its warmth will dissipate. Authenticity is the key to letting this central part within us shine. It is important to realize that there is no darkness, only absence of light. At the core, we are all equally as much a hero worthy of being center stage and worthy of expressing themselves freely. We only have to remove all the inhibitions and restraints around our sun and one can't help but shine as brightly as the center of the cosmos. We are all tiny little centers of the universe.

However, when you look directly into the sun, you will be blinded. If you are too preoccupied with your own ego, too focused on yourself as a separate individual, you will be blind to the spiritual truth of who you are – you are not separate from anything in this cosmos. You are a reflection of the whole and the whole is a reflection of you. You are not just the hero, but also the storyteller. To put it in Joseph Campbell's words, "we are living myth". When you get too close to the sun, you will get burned. When you try to define yourself, you are limiting yourself. When you try to carve out this identity of yours, getting closer and closer to a clear-cut definition of yourself, you realize that this is not you. The truth is, just like a quantum particle, you are all things potentially. The part reflects the whole.

Life is not about finding yourself – you are right here.
Life is not about creating yourself – you already exist.
A lot of people try to carve out an identity for themselves, to define themselves, when all they have to do is just be. The only thing left to arriving is realizing you are already there.

"No one is you and that is your power."
Dave Grohl

☉ Sun in ♈ Aries

Personality has an initiating nature, expresses individuality and willpower directly. This placement makes one identify as a hero, who courageously and competitively goes after what they want.

☉ Sun in ♉ Taurus

Personality has a sensual nature, expresses individuality and willpower stubbornly. This placement makes one identify as savorer, who enjoys a secure foundation of finances, values and physical pleasures.

☉ Sun in ♊ Gemini

Personality has a curious nature, expresses individuality and willpower wittily. This placement makes one identify as a student, who is in a constant exchange of information and thus always learning.

☉ Sun in ♋ Cancer

Personality has a sensitive nature, expresses individuality and willpower in a nurturing way or in a way that demands nurturing. This placement makes one identify as a motherly or childlike figure – or both.

☉ Sun in ♌ Leo

Personality has a dramatic nature, expresses individuality and willpower generously. This placement makes one identify as an entertainer and a king or queen, who both gives and expects to receive love and adoration.

☉ Sun in ♍ Virgo

Personality has a sober nature, expresses individuality and willpower pragmatically. This placement makes one identify as a thorough and chaste perfectionist as well as a helpful servant to others.

☉ Sun in ♎ Libra

Personality has a diplomatic nature, expresses individuality and willpower in a cultivated and other-oriented way. This placement makes one identify as an aesthete and a peacemaker.

☉ Sun in ♏ Scorpio

Personality has a powerful nature, expresses individuality and willpower intensely, sometimes manipulatively. This placement makes one identify as a taboo-breaker who seeks the truth.

☉ Sun in ♐ Sagittarius

Personality has a jovial nature, expresses individuality and willpower expansively and optimistically. This placement makes one identify as a teacher, or even a guru – one is constantly sharing their wisdom.

☉ Sun in ♑ Capricorn

Personality has a reliable nature, expresses individuality and willpower responsibly. This placement makes one identify as the guardian of law and order, a kind of patriarch.

☉ Sun in ♒ Aquarius

Personality has an individualistic nature, expresses individuality and willpower innovatively. This placement makes one identify as a humanitarian, who is focused on personal and collective liberation.

☉ Sun in ♓ Pisces

Personality has an intuitive nature, expresses individuality and willpower passively. This placement makes one identify as a savior or savee, who escapes into love, art or other drugs.

☉ Sun in 1st House

Seeks to express individuality and be special in their persona, puts great importance into the area of self and at succeeding and being recognized in that area. This placement makes one expressive and confident – it makes one put themselves "out there", show initiative.

☉ Sun in 2nd House

Seeks to express individuality and be special in their resources, puts great importance into the area of finances and values and at succeeding and being recognized in that area. This placement makes one feel secure in their identity and therefore enjoys physical pleasures.

☉ Sun in 3rd House

Seeks to express individuality and be special in information exchange, puts great importance into the area of communication and at succeeding and being recognized in that area. This placement makes one chatty, eager to learn and locally connected.

☉ Sun in 4th House

Seeks to express individuality and be special at home, puts great importance into the area of privacy and nurturing their soul and at succeeding and being recognized in that area. This placement makes one rather withdrawn and makes one stick to their roots or heritage.

☉ Sun in 5th House

Seeks to express individuality and be special in who they

are, puts great importance into the area of creativity and at succeeding and being recognized in that area. This placement makes one playful and childlike and express oneself theatrically. They are said to be the "favorite child", often the only child as well – either way, they received a lot of attention.

☉ Sun in 6th House

Seeks to express individuality and be special in daily routine, puts great importance into the area of work and at succeeding and being recognized in that area. This placement makes one industrious and tidy.

☉ Sun in 7th House

Seeks to express individuality and be special in interpersonal relationships, puts great importance into the area of negotiating and collaborating with others and at succeeding and being recognized in that area. This placement makes one dependent and other-oriented.

☉ Sun in 8th House

Seeks to express individuality and be special in their personal power, puts great importance into the area of intimacy with others and at succeeding and being recognized in that area. This placement makes one constantly transform and refine themselves and be interested in occult studies, conspiracies or other kinds of research.

☉ Sun in 9th House

Seeks to express individuality and be special in their higher education, wisdom or belief systems puts great importance into the area of personal development and at succeeding and being recognized in that area. This placement makes one a globetrotter, someone who is open to new experiences and always wants to expand their personal, religious/ideological and academic horizons.

☉ Sun in 10th House

Seeks to express individuality and be special in their career, puts great importance into the area of their public image and at succeeding and being recognized in that area. This placement makes one ambitious, image-consious and success-driven.

☉ Sun in 11th House

Seeks to express individuality and be special in their worldly contributions, puts great importance into the area of social networking and at succeeding and being recognized in that area. This placement makes one collegial and have big dreams and visions.

☉ Sun in 12th House

Seeks to express individuality and be special in their spiritual devotion, puts great importance into the area of escapism and usually does not seek a lot of recognition. This placement makes one passive and driven into isolation at times. However, these individuals are also very empathetic and selfless and might be psychic.

"My life doesn't start until..."

Sun in 1st House: I am born! I am always living in the now!

Sun in 2nd House: I have a safe foundation! I can only live as soon as I feel financially secure and provided for!

Sun in 3rd House: I have someone to talk to! Or something to learn! I hate boredom!

Sun in 4th House: I am home! Either physically or within myself. I need emotional safety!

Sun in 5th House: I am having fun! What's the point of anything if it's not a game?

Sun in 6th House: I finished everything from my to-do list! Work comes first, I have to be organized and productive before I can worry about anything else!

Sun in 7th House: I am in a relationship! I love love and I need to share my life with someone before anything else!

Sun in 8th House: I have transformed myself on a profound level! I need to retreat into my emotional depths and gain personal power before I can do anything else effectively.

Sun in 9th House: I know the truth! I need a philosophy, ideology, religion, or scientific worldview to follow. Until then, how do I know whether I am doing the right thing?

Sun in 10th House: I have made a name for myself! When I have a successful career, then I can worry about other stuff!

Sun in 11th House: I am with my friends! Being within a supportive network that shares my vision is the first thing I have to achieve before I can do anything else. At first, I need them!

Sun in 12th House: I am enlightened! Life is an illusion! I will isolate myself until I break through the barriers of mere mundane existence! Goodbye world!

MOON

*"Your relationship with your mother
is your relationship with the universe."*
Teal Swan

The influence the moon exerts on our earth can easily be seen through the tides of the ocean - pulling it in and pushing it out. The moon influences us humans as well - There's the term *lunatic,* which refers to people who are insane or who have gone crazy.
We have known for ages that we, as humans, are influenced by the moon. Some say that this is because our bodies are mostly made up of water and if the moon controls the water in the oceans, it controls the water in our bodies as well. Your moon sign does not indicate how insane you are but rather who you are when you let all your walls down, when you lose your rational mind and social mask and you simply let your emotions take over.

The moon expresses itself naturally, the sun is focused will. While the sun is our doing, the moon is our being. Cancer is the zodiac sign ruled by the moon. If you look at a crab, its bones are on the outside, so it shows that soft and very personal and vulnerable part within us. Crabs are guarded and defensive, just like our inner moon. Walking sideways to avoid conflict, criticism, and blame. Within our moon, we find that fearful child that does not want to get hurt, that wants to be safe.

The main keyword many associate with the astrological moon is "emotions" or "feelings". It is also connected to our mood swings, similar to the tides of the ocean. This is a quite unconscious part of us, that usually only comes out in immediate reactions and statements made before we could think about them. It shows emotionally charged impulses, the part of you people see when you have an emotional outburst, of either good or bad nature. It might even surprise yourself. This is where your true core comes out.

The sign of the moon expresses what our main motivations are. It describes what we want and need in order to feel comfortable, safe, and loved.
I love Donna Cunningham's approach of describing our natal moon sign as our emotional climate and the signs the moon passes through throughout the days and weeks of everyday life as the emotional weather.

Your moon sign shows how you generally carry yourself emotionally, how you respond to life on an emotional and intuitive level. Your moon sign is also your personality as a child because at an early age, you haven't build up any walls yet, you always act according to spontaneous, emotional responses. The moon in your horoscope represents your inner child, your emotional world that needs to be nurtured and that wants to feel comfortable and at home. We all have an emotionally needy child within us to some degree. One that wants to reach for help and support like a baby reaching for their mother. Many of us ignore and abandon this inner child; silence it. We keep looking outside for something to fulfill us, when all we have to do is turn inside to our inner child to regain emotional health.

Self-care is not selfish; it is absolutely necessary and essential. It is crucial to take care of that inner child. You probably heard the term "be your own best friend", but in my opinion, an even better piece of advice is to "be your own best parent". To not tell yourself to suck it up like an adult and allow yourself to be sad, be vulnerable, nap, cry, ask for help, and be nurtured. Before we can nurture others, we first have to nurture ourselves. I first heard about this analogy from Osho: All trees have to be selfish. They have to suck up water through their roots, soak up the sunshine with their leaves, and do everything to nurture their own wellbeing and growth. Only then can they give fruits for us to eat and shade for us to sit in. It is the same with people. Remember that there's a little vulnerable and needy child within you – nurture and parent it. Don't abandon it.

"It is never too late to have a happy childhood."
Tom Robbins

The moon rules the stomach – the organ that helps us take in physical nurturing in the form of food. The moon is both food for the body and food for the soul. This is why the moon is exalted in the sign Taurus. The cliché representation of a stereotypical Taurus person is someone who is greedy and constantly indulging in luxuries and especially lots of food. That is because this zodiac sign rules material wealth in the form of physical comfort and riches as well as comfort food. Taurus has the biggest capacity of enjoying sensual pleasures. The reason the moon is exalted when in Taurus is because here it can experience the full safety and security of being physically provided for – enjoying the warm breast of the mother, the soft fuzzy blanket, the delicious food… Lunar Taurus stands for the ability to be patient and calm because you know that you will always be provided for. Even if you do not have a mother, everyone belongs to Gaia, mother earth. Mother earth is constantly giving to us, unrestrictedly and without asking anything back from us – like a mother with her baby. This is the resourcefulness of a security blanket that will always catch us and nurture us no matter what.

The moon is connected to our family, the need to have a family or to connect with it – especially the mother. This luminary is the classic symbol of womanhood. Archetypically, it depicts the three-fold goddess of the virgin (new moon), the pregnant mother (full moon) and the crone or old wise woman (waning moon). This symbolism relates closely to the menstrual cycle (which takes about twenty-eight days, just like the moon cycle) and the womb – the feeling of being safe, nurtured and at home within the literal womb, the lap of the mother, a mother figure or any safe space amongst people who love us.

It is not just our mother in the literal sense, but also how we see and experience female figures in general. Especially female teachers and other women, who, throughout our lives, are a substitute for our real mother. It shows how they relate to the feminine principle of retreating inwards, nurturing and being nurtured. Next to the Venus sign, which shows a romantic and sexual attraction towards women, more of an infatuation, the moon sign shows the type of woman someone would bond with most deeply and settle down with. It is kind of true, then, that men fall for women who subconsciously remind them of their mothers – because they look for that type of nurturing and love they have experienced when they were little. Therefore, it is important to parent yourself as to not look for emotional fulfillment in a maternal figure. We have to overcome this infantile emotional abuse of wanting our partners and spouses to give us what our parents and we ourselves failed to give to us.

All matriarchal values are connected to this archetype, such as intuition and gut feelings that are especially strong in but not limited to women. This inner knowing and wisdom stems from the unconscious relation to life that was built through our relationship with our mother. As infants, our mother was our life. Whatever she exuded, we absorbed, and is now our way of sensing intuitively. Someone with a Virgo moon might have had a very anxious mother that was quite tense and always sensed when something was wrong with her baby. Now this child grows up to be very health-conscious, detail-oriented and thorough themselves, because this emotional atmosphere was so deeply absorbed when they were little.

Since the actual moon merely shines because it reflects the light of the sun, the moon in our horoscope also shows a part of us that is more reflective; retreats, rather than goes out consciously and directly. All reflections are slightly distorted and the moon filters the light it reflects through early childhood experiences and the emotional attitudes we have. Our past and upbringing, where we come from, these roots and our heritage, is what shape our moon personality. Therefore, the sign the moon is in gives clues to what makes us feel *at home* – both in the world and within ourselves.

This homeliness and domestic nature of us is a part of our psyche, which supports the notion of "you are your own home", meaning that we have to arrive within. The moon stands for comfort and attachment, for the feeling of coming home physically or emotionally, that feeling of safety that babies have in the womb. We express our moon personality around people we're close with, when we're comfortable. That's why, in a lot of schools of astrology, the moon sign is considered more important in one's personality than your sun sign - is your innermost, intimate self. It is usually said that this is our personality we show our family (assuming we are close and comfortable with them), or anyone that is really *familiar* to us.

While the sun stands for the present and the future, the moon stands for the present and the past – a retrospective attitude. The past and the wisdom gained from it as well as sentimentality and nostalgia attached to that past color the moon in our horoscopes. Emotional experiences from the past also influence our defenses and how guarded we are or aren't. Since the moon can be summed up as "reactions" rather than the solar "action", you could say that these stem from unconscious memory from the past that conditioned us in a certain way. The moon sign also paints a picture of our temper tantrums (together with mars) or our emotional sensitivities – it shows what gets to us, what *hits home*, because things from the past still shape our habitual reactions.

Since the moon is our home, the house your moon resides in could be considered your comfort zone - where you instinctively feel drawn to and what seems natural to you, where you feel nurtured and want to retreat to in order to regain emotional balance. It's vital to retreat into these comfort zones from time to time. Even though it's important to stretch comfort zones, to put ourselves out there and to expand our horizons, we should also make time to recharge and nurture ourselves.
We naturally feel drawn to and intrigued by these life areas and they have a big influence on our moods and make us emotionally vulnerable. These areas of life also fluctuate a lot, together with the phases of the moon and the tides of the ocean.

☽ Moon in ♈ Aries

Fiery emotional climate, mood swings are sudden and fade just as quickly, nurtures and seeks to be nurtured in a protective and chivalrous way, feels comfortable in energetic surroundings and atmospheres. This placement makes one direct and assertive.

☽ Moon in ♉ Taurus

Sensual emotional climate, mood swings are slow and steady, nurtures and seeks to be nurtured in a physical way (hugs, food,..), feels comfortable in natural and quiet surroundings and atmospheres. This placement makes one stubborn, but also a bastion of calm.

☽ Moon in ♊ Gemini

Buzzing emotional climate, mood swings are rationalized, nurtures and seeks to be nurtured in a rational way, feels comfortable in stimulating surroundings and atmospheres. This placement makes one chatty and easily bored.

☽ Moon in ♋ Cancer

Sensitive emotional climate, is moody, nurtures and seeks to be nurtured in a maternal way, feels comfortable in domestic and private surroundings and atmospheres. This placement makes one take things personally very easily but also very sensitive to how others feel.

☽ Moon in ♌ Leo

Sunny emotional climate, mood swings are dramatic, nurtures and seeks to be nurtured by being adored and showing adoration, feels comfortable in playful surroundings and atmospheres. This placement makes one a natural entertainer and an eternal child.

☽ **Moon in ♍ Virgo**

Calm emotional climate, mood swings are dealt with effectively, nurtures and seeks to be nurtured in a pragmatic way, feels comfortable in clean and tidy surroundings and atmospheres. This placement makes one have street smarts and always know how to react to situations sensibly.

☽ **Moon in ♎ Libra**

Sociable emotional climate, mood swings are balanced but can be too rational, nurtures and seeks to be nurtured in a friendly and just way, feels comfortable in companionable surroundings and atmospheres. This placement makes one very fair and polite.

☽ **Moon in ♏ Scorpio**

Deep and powerful emotional climate, mood swings are intense, nurtures and seeks to be nurtured in an intimate way, feels comfortable in surroundings and atmospheres in which one is in control. This placement makes one brood on moods.

☽ **Moon in ♐ Sagittarius**

Optimistic emotional climate, mood swings are exaggerated, nurtures and seeks to be nurtured in an uplifting, motivating way, feels comfortable in educational or cosmopolitan surroundings and atmospheres. This placement makes one enthusiastic and self-righteous.

☽ Moon in ♑ Capricorn

Mature emotional climate, mood swings are managed practically, nurtures and seeks to be nurtured with respect, feels comfortable in professional surroundings and atmospheres. This placement makes one naturally take on responsibility and, rather than being sensitive and naïve, be quite distanced from their emotions.

☽ Moon in ♒ Aquarius

Objective and intellectual emotional climate, mood swings are rebellious or unpredictable, nurtures and seeks to be nurtured in a collegial way, feels comfortable in social and progressive surroundings (like demonstrations) and atmospheres. This placement makes one be humanitarian.

☽ Moon in ♓ Pisces

Sensitive emotional climate, mood swings are intuitive, nurtures and seeks to be nurtured in an unconditionally loving way, feels comfortable in quiet or even solitary surroundings and atmospheres. This placement makes one trust others easily and be compassionate and spiritual.

☽ Moon in 1st House

Naturally feels drawn to presenting themselves, feels comfortable and at home in their own skin, experiences lots of up and downs in their personal identity. This placement makes one wear their heart on their sleeves.

☽ Moon in 2nd House

Naturally feels drawn to sensual pleasures, feels comfortable and at home when they are financially secure, experiences lots of up and downs in area of their wealth on a material and personal level. This placement makes one quite indulgent and nurtured by physical matters.

☽ Moon in 3rd House

Naturally feels drawn to learning and sharing information, feels comfortable and at home when communicating their thoughts, experiences lots of up and downs in area of early education and siblings (if they have any). This placement makes one learn easily, but only when in the mood for it.

☽ Moon in 4th House

Naturally feels drawn to retreating into themselves or their physical home, feels comfortable and at home within their being, experiences lots of up and downs in their home. This placement makes one emotionally attached to their heritage.

☽ Moon in 5th House

Naturally feels drawn to creative self-expression, feels comfortable and at home when entertaining others, experiences lots of up and downs in area of love, fun, and creativity. This placement makes one childlike and playful.

☽ Moon in 6th House

Naturally feels drawn to routine, feels comfortable and at home when being organized and productive, experiences lots of up and downs in area of work. This placement makes one feel at ease when they are being "a gear in the machine" – healthy and contributing through their work.

☽ Moon in 7th House

Naturally feels drawn to relationships, feels comfortable and at home when they can share their life with a partner, experiences lots of up and downs in area of partnerships. This placement makes one emotionally dependent but also very devoted.

☽ Moon in 8th House

Naturally feels drawn to that which is hidden, feels comfortable and at home in the world of the occult and taboos, experiences lots of up and downs in area of personal transformation. This placement makes one go through extreme and intense phases of insight and growth.

☽ Moon in 9th House

Naturally feels drawn to higher education and religion, feels comfortable and at home in the whole word and its diverse cultures, experiences lots of up and downs in area of personal growth and their philosophy of the world. This placement makes one need to have a worldview to hold on to for emotional security.

☽ Moon in 10th House

Naturally feels drawn to the public eye and into visibility, feels comfortable and at home when they are being recognized, experiences lots of up and downs in area of their career. This placement makes one have their emotional wellbeing be tied to how well they are perceived – to their reputation.

☽ Moon in 11th House

Naturally feels drawn to groups of people, feels comfortable and at home around friends, experiences lots of up and downs in their social circle. This placement makes one collegial and conscious of the whole group and its connection.

☽ Moon in 12th House

Naturally feels drawn to their own subconscious, feels comfortable and at home in isolation, tends to hide their emotions even from themselves. This placement can make one reclusive.

MERCURY

"God is a comedian playing to an audience afraid to laugh."
Voltaire

Mercury rules thinking, logic and communication – this whole principle seems to be trivial, especially in the eyes of modern western culture, where being literate and being in constant communication with the world is so natural. I remember that when I first got into astrology, I thought that Mercury was boring and unimportant. However, the Sanskrit name for Mercury is actually *Buddha*, the title for an enlightened person. It is connected to real *knowing*, not just basic facts and trivia. Mercury is our desire to learn and understand – that spark that makes us interested in collecting information on a certain topic, that part within us that processes all the little pieces, connects the dots and comes up with ideas and opinions concerning certain topics. He is an unattached observer, a scientist.

Mercurian energy exists all around us, in the realm of thoughts, surrounding us like air (because thoughts are energy), buzzing through our nervous system (that Mercury rules). This is the part within us that juggles a lot of things at once, that wants to multi-task, has too many tabs open and needs constant entertainment and flow of information, preferably from several sides or sources at once. Mercury is the fastest moving planet, he is the messenger god, always sprinting around, taking in and giving out information.

This planet also shows how we take in all information we are presented with about our reality, how we process it. This heavily influences our perception of the world and how we experience it mentally.

Mercury is the planet of dialogue. The word dialogue contains "dia–", meaning "two". Two people in interaction with each other, the human mind in conversation with the world. Dialogue not only describes the interaction of two people, the back and forth of talking to each other. We are, each of us, constantly in dialogue with the world around us, we receive information and send out information. Always. Even on the most unconscious level, in a non-verbal way, there is a constant dialogue between us and the world. In medical astrology, Mercury rules the lungs, arms and hands – all existing in twos and the main means of communication next to the face.

Language and articulation, the system of symbols and sounds that is written and spoken language, is what Mercury is about. It is connected to the element air, because vibrating air produces sound, vibrating vocal chords produce speech. Whether spoken, written, or in another medium, Mercury is about giving voice to something. If you were taught to be quiet, your breathing will be flat and the muscles around your chest, jaw and neck tight. What this mirrors in your body is the suppression and keeping in of your thoughts and opinions.

The lesson of Mercury is that of finding your voice. Sharing your unique thoughts and ideas is important, because the combination of individual perspectives bring us closer to the truth, the sharing of our perceptions of reality connect us with others.

Imagine never having learned a language. How would you think? How did you think before you could speak, write or read? By giving something a name, associating words with it, it takes on specific forms in our mind, it changes shape. Words and thoughts shape reality. Change your words and you change your world. We give gender to things that don't have gender in language, linguistics shape culture and vice versa. Talk about the pen being mightier than the sword. Do you ever think that if you had a different name, you would be a different person? Do you ever notice how we associate traits with names? Someone says "My friend Marcus will be there, too". You hear the name Marcus and in your mind, you have already created a picture of him. We highly identify with our names, so they must shape the way we identify as people – they must shape our inner sun. Mercury is never more than 28° away from the sun, it is the planet closest to the sun – we shape our identity through communication and language.

In mythology, Mercurian gods, such as the Greek Hermes and the Norse Loki, are tricksters – in their minds, there is no right or wrong, no true or false – they try to outwit people (and pretty much always succeed), they simply want to play around and collect data. One of my favorite mythological stories is about Hermes, who, after having been given birth to, steals Apollo's cattle. The first thing he does as a little baby fresh out of the womb is to take away his brothers cows. He actually didn't use the umbilical cord as a lasso, but instead made the cows walk backwards as to lead people in the wrong direction – very clever and snarky little infant he was. Any person with a strong influence of Mercury in their natal chart will portray these trickster qualities. They're usually youthful, playful and fun, and can turn anything into a game.

Mercury personified would be nervously tapping their foot, playing with a pen in their hand, interrupting conversations to get out a sudden idea immediately. Mercury is witty and eloquent, never takes themselves (or anything, for that matter) seriously, and winks at you when making another clever joke. On Mount Olympus, Mercury is the messenger of the Greek Gods. He rules short distance travel and his job is to connect point A and point B, whether that be two places, two people or two pieces of information. Being the closest to the sun, it moves the quickest out of all the planets in our solar system, symbolizing the quick wit and the swift and clever intellect that Mercury represents.

A person with strong Mercury influences is not necessarily opinionated in the sense that they highly believe in certain worldviews and hold them holy – that is Jupiter. Mercury simply throws and opinion in the room to get a conversation going – to see other peoples viewpoints, learn from them, compare them with their own. Mercury never holds onto beliefs. He simply thinks with no personal attachment, no moral judgment. To have personal and emotional stuff intervene in trying to see the world objectively is not in his interest. Mercury rules Gemini, the sign of twins. Mercury can see two opposing points of view simultaneously and can see them to be equally correct and valid. The truth of the universe is that of oneness, contrast exists merely to aid in the human experience. Mercury knows that opposites are the same thing in differing degree, night and day are opposite sides of the same coin – Mercury takes seemingly contrasting points and combines them. He does not judge. He isn't on any side and has no ideology. Geminis especially seem to often hold two apparently mutually negating opinions at the same time. That is what defines the trickster archetype. Beyond good or evil, he does things for the hell of it – to see what is possible, to see how the human mind works and how one can trick it and play with it.

Riddles, trivia quizzes, and games are all associated with Mercury, because they are playful ways to learn. Early education, our siblings and our neighborhood are our first contacts with the world outside of our parents (sun and moon) and they also belong to the sphere of Mercury. Business, commerce, and marketing are also ruled by Mercury, since trade, selling products, selling ideas, bargaining, and talking someone into something are all Mercurian things – connected to mind, intellect, wit, and connections.

Mercury also rules humor. There's a whole science about what makes something funny, but punch lines or slapstick humor are usually so hilarious because they make us see different possibilities of thinking or acting. Our minds love to learn and when they are presented with a new possibility of seeing the world and interacting with it, they find so much enjoyment in it that it makes us laugh! Humor is the best way to learn and Gemini is the master of infotainment.

Mercury is androgynous, since he represents duality in all its forms. This is also shown in his rulership over one masculine and one feminine sign – Gemini and Virgo. This gives the planet of logic and intellect two very distinct qualities, one which is airy and one which is earthy, one which is mental and one which is practical.

The purpose of the Gemini Mercury is to keep asking questions, inquiring, staying curious and remembering that there is no absolute truth. Gemini Mercury always says "Yes but no", being aware of the ambiguity of all things, of their duality. Gemini doubts everything, stays open to being wrong and learning that way. Like a little child, Gemini never stops asking questions. "Why? And why is that? But why?" That is how, gradually, Gemini knows a little about everything and is really adaptable. This is the archetype of the twin tricksters – the couple of mischievous young boys or girls who play pranks and trick you.

The Virgo Mercury, on the other hand, is a lot more practical and physical, prefers to use the hands rather than the brain and to understand things through application. The Virgo intellect works like gears in a machine – everything runs smoothly and almost mechanically. Virgo wants to be a productive and efficient member of society, "do their job" and perfect all physical processes like a robot. That is why this sign is associated with apprenticeship and craftsmanship and anything else that requires the learning and using of certain skills. It also rules routine, work and daily tasks and responsibilities. When saying that the purpose of the zodiac sign Virgo is to judge, discriminate and pigeon-hole, it sounds really negative. However, this is a crucial part of the zodiac wheel. Virgo rules the digestive system and much like this anatomical equivalent, Virgo sorts out and keeps that which has a pragmatic purpose, it makes the most efficient and productive use of everything and is quite the perfectionist in the process of always refining, analyzing and sorting out.

Even though this sign has a really sober quality about it, being ruled by the quickest planet in the solar system can still make it be quite nervous and anxious, particularly when it comes to health. Virgo is associated with hypochondria, showing the sign's fear of not having been thorough, pure, clean, virginal and effective enough. "You reap what you sow" is the motto of this hard-working sign that is associated with the season of harvest.

Mercury is considered to be exalted in Virgo, be at its peak performance, so to say, in this sign. However, there now is a discussion in modern astrology whether Mercury should be considered to be in exaltation in Aquarius instead. In Virgo, Mercury works like a gear in a machine, learning things by heart and in detail, spitting out data like a computer, reproducing information. However, Aquarius is genius. It is non-conventional, it goes against tradition. Mercury in Aquarius is the inventor, the revolutionary. Only when you go against convention, you can actually expand your knowledge beyond that of others, discover something new and make progress.

☿ Mercury in ♈ Aries

Direct style of thinking, likes mental disputes, aggressive opinions, quick witted, simple and uncomplicated mind, spontaneous decision-making or changes of mind.

☿ Mercury in ♉ Taurus

Practical thinker, realistic, reluctant and slow to change opinions, dry, thorough thinking, thick-headed, consistent at best and conservative at worst.

☿ Mercury in ♊ Gemini

Quick wit, objective and adaptable mind, good at connecting random pieces of information, intellectual, great communicator, curious, meditative, mind can be scattered and fickle or trivial.

☿ Mercury in ♋ Cancer

Subjective mind, poetic, intuitive and understanding communicator, imaginative, good (emotional) memory, naïve or non-intellectual, biased.

☿ Mercury in ♌ Leo

Thinks big, dramatic storyteller, creative mind, and animated expression of opinions, might ignore details, can't accept being wrong, gambler, sovereign communicator.

☿ Mercury in ♍ Virgo

Practical thinker, skilled, witty, crafty and good with their hands, very analytical, focus on details, dry and precise, can be prejudiced, nitpicky and petty.

☿ Mercury in ♎ Libra

Fair, charming conversationalist, good judgment, strategic, diplomatic, problems with making decisions, too theoretical at times, avoids conflict with their opinions (does not commit to taking sides).

☿ Mercury in ♏ Scorpio

Black and white thinking, uses "always" or "never" a lot, extreme opinions, deep thoughts, investigative mind, good at research.

☿ Mercury in ♐ Sagittarius

Idealistic, prefers concepts and the big picture over facts and details, open-minded, cosmopolitan, strong beliefs and convictions, moral, dogmatic, lacks critical thinking.

☿ Mercury in ♑ Capricorn

Pragmatic thinker, realistic, high ability for concentration, can keep a great birds-eye-view of structures, lacks creative imagination, conservative, dry and monotone communicator.

☿ Mercury in ♒ Aquarius

Progressive ideas, genius sparks of inspiration, avant-garde opinions or ways of thinking, scientific, detached and objective mind.

☿ Mercury in ♓ Pisces

Talks and thinks in symbols or images, dreamy and intuitive mind, great imagination and poetic self-expression, tends to either deceive or be deceived, lacks objectivity and rationality.

☿ Mercury in 1st House

The mind is preoccupied with how one comes across, intellect is mainly put to use towards defining someone's identity and expressing someone's individuality, clever and communicative.

☿ Mercury in 2nd House

The mind is preoccupied with one's security, intellect is mainly put to use towards managing their wealth, very economical and business-minded.

☿ Mercury in 3rd House

The mind is preoccupied with learning and communication, intellect is mainly put to use towards sharing information with others and building mental connections, very adaptable and witty.

☿ Mercury in 4th House

The mind is preoccupied with one's heritage and past, ideas and intellect are mainly put to use in the way the parents have taught (can be old-fashioned), private about their thoughts.

☿ Mercury in 5th House

The mind is preoccupied with play and self-expression, ideas and intellect are mainly put to use towards fun and games, good with words, flirty, creative, can be a gambler.

☿ Mercury in 6th House

The mind is preoccupied with daily tasks and work, ideas and intellect are mainly put to use towards helping and serving others, detail-oriented and efficient.

☿ Mercury in 7th House

The mind is preoccupied with one's relationships with others, ideas and intellect are mainly put to use towards building connections (setting people up with each other), enjoys debates, rationalizes their partnerships.

☿ Mercury in 8th House

The mind is preoccupied with deep or dark thoughts or subjects, ideas and intellect are mainly put to use towards healing or transformation (could be a great psychologer), curious about that which is taboo, secretive.

☿ Mercury in 9th House

The mind is preoccupied with the big questions of philosophy, ideas and intellect are mainly put to use towards defining a certain worldview or beliefs, intellectual and curious about other cultures.

☿ Mercury in 10th House

The mind is preoccupied with how one comes across and stands publically, ideas and intellect are mainly put to use in their career (could have jobs in writing or speaking), image-conscious.

☿ Mercury in 11th House

The mind is preoccupied with their visions of the future, ideas and intellect are mainly put to use towards the benefit and progression of humanity or the collective, idealistic and forward-thinking.

☿ Mercury in 12th House

The mind is preoccupied with introspection, ideas and intellect are mainly put to use towards selfless acts but also daydreaming, unclear communication, has to be alone to be able to sort out their thoughts.

VENUS

*"I'm going to make everything around me beautiful-
that will be my life."*
Elsie de Wolfe

Venus is the goddess within each of us, regardless of sex and gender. She rules the masculine sign Libra and the feminine sign Taurus. In the air sign Libra, the goddess expresses herself through charming speech, flirts, good taste, manners, fairness, romance, and culture. In the earth sign Taurus, the goddess expresses herself though all sensual pleasures and means of nurturing – music, hugs, blankets, food, scented candles, art, and other kinds of luxury and indulgence. In our charts, Venus describes that part that wishes to experience peace, beauty and pleasure. It is our charming or artistic side that knows how to wrap people around her finger and enchant them. This magnetic feminine allure is represented by the Greek goddess Aphrodite. We each have a piece of this seductive archetype within us and it allows us to draw people into our spell by being beautiful and attractive in our own way.

Venus in an individual's chart shows their desire to be admired, to be someone's object of competition. She makes us want to be attractive and desirable to others. Venus is your own personal aphrodisiac. When put to use effectively, it can cause a Trojan war. What's more is that the goddess of love need not actively pursue what she wants – she simply bats her lashes and has everyone running to open the door for her and carry her bag. Thus, the house of the chart Venus falls into shows the area of life in which we can be charming enough to receive what we desire, while the sign Venus is in shows the unique kind of charm someone possesses.

Since Venus rules Libra, the sign of the scales, it is important for her energy to be in balance. When excessive, Venus can be superficial and perverted, addicted to pleasure and overly indulgent, greedy, lazy, arrogant, and naïve enough to trust and be seduced by everyone effortlessly – the stereotypical "whore" or "gold digger". However, when the Venus energy in a person is weak or suppressed, this entails problems with femininity – both exterior, with actual women and one's ability to get along with or be desired by them, and interior, in one's ability to savor pleasures, see beauty, be charming and negotiate.

Not only does Venus show our relationship to women, but our whole desire to connect with others and our social skills. "Relationships" is a central word for this planet since it describes how we relate to all things and people. Venus is our willingness to make compromises and negotiate with others in order to get along with them; it is our desire to be included and accepted and to find belonging. It is also our readiness to provide this to others, to make them feel welcomed. Libra, the sign ruled by Venus, is symbolized by the scales, the only object in the zodiac. It stands for purely *objective* judgment, justice, fairness, and equality. Venus rules our sense of balance in the body as well, ensuring equilibrium in all areas.

Without Venus, there would be no urge to socialize within us and no need for companionship – and however strongly or weakly a natal Venus is placed in an individual's chart will show their respective ability and need for exactly that – friendships and romance. This planet is all about others and one's relationship to them. Archetypically, Venus is a pacifist, a judge, a referee, a model, an artist, a poet; she sees the beauty in people, shapes, and colors and loves the harmonic interplay of those. At her best, Venus will express herself through such traits as gracefulness, sociability, understanding and selflessness. She teaches us good manners and etiquette by observing others and following their lead. In a way, somebody's Venus sign can show how they connect with others, how they bond and break the ice. A fire Venus might do that through humor or mutual passions, a water Venus through an emotional connection or a shared nostalgia, an air Venus through ideas or opinions and an earth Venus might prefer a more practical approach like a reassuring touch.

The Venus symbol also serves as that of "female", while the Mars symbol also serves as that of "male". In astrology, these planets are associated with archetypal feminine and masculine energies, respectively. They describe opposing principles. Whereas Mars shows our primitive, egocentric animal nature, Venus shows where we cultivate things with others and find pleasure. Through Venus we learn to be civilized, we become part of the civilization. By cultivating a society with others, Venus shows us the pleasures of art, poetry, music, and all the beautiful things that a culture has to offer. When we negotiate with others rather than focusing on ourselves, we are rewarded with the luxuries of a refined, elegant and graceful lifestyle that is anything but primitive and animalistic. The people-loving Venus refuses to see humans as animals and rules that which is unique to intelligent and civilized man: a sense of aesthetic or beauty, manners and politeness, art, and good taste. The traits and qualities of that which we value and desire is indicated by the sign placement of Venus in our charts. It describes our idea of what is aesthetically pleasing, beautiful, and valuable – that which we like and enjoy; our tastes, simply put. Hence, Venus indicates our lifestyle. That which we value is that which we buy. Some say Venus indicates money, but, more precisely, it indicates what we do with our wealth, because it shows what we find pleasure in, and what we are therefore willing to spend our money on.

Venus enjoys comfort and all sensual pleasures. The planet rules our neck and oral tract and both our ability to speak or sing beautifully as well as the taking in of food and drinks. Venus loves pampering herself and can even be over-indulgent. Psychologically, she is connected to the oral phase of our development; that time when both our life and emotional wellbeing was tied to sucking on our mother's breast. Our mother is our first experience of the pleasure of company and closeness to others. When there was a lack of physical contact with a caretaker in infancy, one can develop an oral personality structure which makes that person be very dependent on others, desperately trying to be loved and held. These people thus can have problems growing out of this infantile and emotionally immature attitude towards relationships, looking for a type of surrogate mother.

Still, the desire to love and be loved is a central part in the human experience. Venus shows our ability to give and receive all forms of love and affection. As is etymologically indicated, the veins in our body are ruled by Venus. They deliver the blood towards our heart, while Venus delivers the love to our non-physical heart. Being the planet of relationships, cooperation, and togetherness, the sign that Venus is in shows someone's "love language" – how they express affection and how they expect to receive it from others; through which channel. We tend to only "understand" love when it's in the same "language"; that is why air and fire Venus' are said to be compatible interchangeably, as well as earth and water Venus'. If Venus signs aren't compatible, we might not feel another person's love, because it does not come through the medium that we'd expect. Our Venus sign shows our idea of what love should be. It is also your unique charm and shows what you do to attract others. The Venus in our charts simply wants to be loved, complimented, desired, and pampered.

This planet is exalted in Pisces, where affection no longer is a give-and-take. One completely spends their love and gives everything to an idealized version of a person.

Here, love becomes unconditional and turns into complete devotion and sacrifice.

"You are so unconditionally loved and supported that you are allowed to feel unsupported and not loved."
Bashar

In his classic work "The Art of Loving", Erich Fromm writes that love has taken on a capitalistic character – only invest enough to make profit, always aim for lucrative business. According to Fromm, rather than love being random and a nice thing once we find an object we can direct it towards, it is an art to be learned. If you can't love everyone, he says, you have not yet mastered this art. But we are all so afraid of being the one who loves more. "Where's the fair trade?" we ask, terrified of making a bad deal, acting like love is a limited resource. I think that the problem with feeling like love is finite is not only our fear of giving, but also our inability of receiving it. We might not be able to fully appreciate and feel the love already available to us. Our symbolic heart spaces are tightened, letting only little love in and out. When you're hyperventilating, there may be plenty of air all around, but you can only let very little of it into your lungs, getting you close to suffocating. When your heart space is tightened, you are constantly starved of love, even though there might be lots of it – so you start treating it greedily, like there is only so much to go around and you have to get your fair share of it. "Just open yourself up to love" is as easily said and as ridiculously hard to do as telling someone who is choking to "Just breathe".

To truly love, love can't be exclusive to a certain object or recipient. We have to become a vessel for the whole love of the universe to flow through unrestrictedly.

Everyone reflects back to us aspects of ourselves – consciously or unconsciously. The Venus symbol is the hand mirror – in it we see our own face reflected back to us. We can only truly love other people to the same degree that we love ourselves and vice versa. How much we value ourselves is reflected in what we let ourselves receive. You can only fill your own cup so much. When you allow others to help you fill your cup, let yourself truly receive their love, your cup can start spilling over on others.

The hardest person to love and accept is yourself, because you are with yourself in every single embarrassing moment, you see all your bad hair days, all your little chubby bits, you remember all your failures and regrets, you know all your flaws and weaknesses. To love yourself is true compassion. To love yourself is to love everyone else – because they are all reflections of you.

♀Venus in ♈ Aries

Expresses affection directly and is straight-forward about their feelings, idea of love as being a conquest or a trophy, ideal of femininity as being assertive and independent, attracted to someone with leadership qualities, individual charm comes through their wild and childlike spirit.

♀Venus in ♉ Taurus

Expresses affection physically, idea of love as being a long-term commitment and pleasure, ideal of femininity as being sensual and grounded, attracted to reliable and pragmatic types, individual charm lies in their natural earthiness.

♀Venus in ♊ Gemini

Expresses affection verbally, idea of love as being exciting and providing variety, ideal of femininity as being clever and funny, attracted to an interesting mind, individual charm comes through their flirty and witty speech.

♀Venus in ♋ Cancer

Expresses affection in a maternal way, idea of love as being nurturing, ideal of femininity as being romantic and family-oriented, attracted to someone who makes them feel at home and safe or someone who needs them, individual charm comes through their empathic and emotional side.

♀Venus in ♌ Leo

Expresses affection theatrically, idea of love as being a melodramatic romance, ideal of femininity as being proud and generous, attracted to a confident and entertaining person, individual charm comes through their joie de vivre, their love of life.

♀Venus in ♍ Virgo

Expresses affection through helping and serving others, idea of love as being a perfect working together of people, ideal of femininity as being refined and modest, attracted to hardworking and humble people, individual charm comes through their dry intellect, skills and capabilities.

♀Venus in ♎ Libra

Expresses affection romantically and with charm, idea of love as being a partnership of equals, ideal of femininity as being tasteful and well-mannered, attracted to someone who is charming and cultivated, individual charm lies in their elegance and sociability.

♀Venus in ♏ Scorpio

Expresses affection cautiously (to avoid being the one who loves more), idea of love as being an intense and intimate union, ideal of femininity as being mysterious and a bit dark, attracted to honesty and power, individual charm comes through their ability to look right through you while remaining impenetrable themselves.

♀Venus in ♆ Sagittarius

Expresses affection through the idealization of a person, idea of love as being an adventure that expands your horizons, ideal of femininity as being intellectual and cosmopolitan, attracted to philosophical and educated people, individual charm comes through their carefree optimism.

♀Venus in ♑ Capricorn

Expresses affection through loyalty and integrity, idea of love as being something that you earn, ideal of femininity as being ambitious and successful, attracted to those of high status and with clear goals, individual charm comes through their air of authority.

♀Venus in ♒ Aquarius

Expresses affection casually (like a friend), idea of love as being a companionship with personal freedom, ideal of femininity as being quirky and independent, attracted to those who are a bit weird or rebellious, individual charm comes through their coolness and intellectual detachment.

♀Venus in ♓ Pisces

Expresses affection unconditionally, idea of love as being a spiritual experience, ideal of femininity as being mystic and otherworldly, attracted to the artistic and poetic or someone who either needs saving by them or saves them, individual charm comes through their imaginative mind and selfless heart.

♀ Venus in 1st House

Uses their charm as part of their identity, finds pleasure in presenting themselves to the world, is open to compromise and collaboration and takes in the role of the peacemaker, is polite and sometimes too nice.

♀ Venus in 2nd House

Good taste and an affinity to luxury, finds pleasure in material things and money (may be very indulgent and materialistic), money as a symbol of affection – both given and received.

♀ Venus in 3rd House

Uses their charm in their speech and/or writing, finds pleasure in conversations or studying and reading, is open to compromise and collaboration on an intellectual level – a great debater.

♀ Venus in 4th House

Uses their charm to create a beautiful environment, finds pleasure by being at home with the people closest to them, is open to compromise and collaboration with their family – may come from an especially peaceful home and is attached to their roots.

♀ Venus in 5th House

Uses their charm in their creative self-expression (artistic abilities and a flashy self-presentation), finds pleasure in flirts and romance, focused on their own pleasure and glory more so than that of others.

♀ Venus in 6th House

Uses their charm in their job (may be popular with co-workers or help people for a living), finds pleasure in routine and a healthy life, good organizational skills, is open to compromise and collaboration at work (good team worker).

♀ Venus in 7th House

Uses their charm to get along and negotiate with others, finds pleasure in partnerships and romance, is open to compromise and collaboration with equals (in romantic and business partnerships), sometimes too dependent and compromising.

♀ Venus in 8th House

Sees beauty in the morbid and dark (sometimes to the point of being perverted), finds pleasure in intimate bonds and sex, very passionate, can gain financial advantages through their partners.

♀ Venus in 9th House

Finds the meaning of life in relationships, finds pleasure in education and philosophizing, is open to compromise and collaboration when it comes to their worldview – may adjust to other's beliefs or talk others into theirs.

♀ Venus in 10th House

Uses their charm in their career (for a favorable public image), finds pleasure in creating a reputation and success for themselves, is known for being open to compromise and collaboration and therefore very popular – might use this consciously to their benefit.

♀ Venus in 11th House

Uses their charm among friends, finds pleasure in the company of those who share their vision, is open to compromise and collaboration in groups of people (great networker, connects people with each other).

♀ Venus in 12th House

Their charm is not expressed freely but rather hidden, finds pleasure in escapism and alone time, craves a fantasy romance and is very sacrificial and charitable, may have secret love affairs.

MARS

"Decide that you want it more than you're afraid of it."
Bill Cosby

The red planet still has a bit of a bad reputation since being labeled "malefic" in traditional astrology. Mars is the planet of war, associated aggression and violence. He is the source of the martial arts and brings out the savage and animal side in us humans. Being the counterpart to the civilized and cultured Venus, Mars is primitive and cruel, egoistic in his intentions, and marks his territory rather than looking for connection with others.

The combative Mars always takes the most direct path, ramming the horns of its ruling sign Aries through the wall. Anatomically, Mars rules the head, so this planet really lives by the motto "head first", bursting into new adventures, regardless of the consequences, in the heat of the moment. This is the planet of birth; the very purpose of Mars is to be a pioneer and trailblazer, to give birth to new ideas and projects and lead them on. He is that first push of energy that gets something going, he goes head first through the birth canal (that imagery is a bit crass, but so is Mars. And bloody). Mars is always ready for departure, never afraid to burn bridges so they may light his way. Primitive actually merely means "coming first", which describes Mars perfectly – he always wants to be first. He loves competition and is always looking for conflict. That is why our house placement of Mars can indicate where we tend to be irritable and quickly pick up fights. In that area of life, we are highly competitive – there is no Venusian "together", only Martial "against". Mars shows where we do not accept compromise. He doesn't do something for the fun of it, he does it to win. Much like the famous Aries Caesar who coined the phrase "veni, vidi, vici", Mars says "What's the point if I can't win? That's why I am here – I come, I see, I win."

Because being the best or being first is so important to the god of war, he loves challenges and dares. The Greek name for this god is Ares and, weirdly (or not so weirdly), many terms associated with him begin with an 'a' – anger, aggression, assertion, attack,… He rules everything that is violent and destructive, including war, battle, rivalry, and fights. Another cool coincidence (or rather, synchronicity) is that Mars rules iron and weapons and that the actual planet Mars is full of iron. That is precisely the reason why it is red – it is rusty.

In our bodies, Mars rules our physical armor, which is our musculature. It aids in both fight and flight, attack and defense. There is a quote by Liza Palmer saying that "Angry is just sad's bodyguard". It is important to realize that there is quite some psychological depth to the Mars in someone's chart. Our instinct to defend ourselves or fight someone stems from us having felt like we have to take on that guarded and combative stance is the first place. Mars makes our will to survive kick in and although he is egoistic, there is usually something that made this necessary, that made us feel like we have to save ourselves in a "life or death" scenario.

Mars catalyzes all kinds of energies and the sign that it is in shows how we act when we get heated up or turned on aggressively, sexually or passionately. This zodiac sign shows what motivates someone and what drives their actions as well as what those actions look like.

Without Mars, there would be no passion and no drive for thrill and adrenaline (another 'a'-word). Mars is our inner daredevil, the wild and untamed warrior or amazon with a go-get-it mentality, who, in the back of our heads, screams "Just do it" or some other war cry. He makes us go after what we want, he makes us chase that which we desire. I was recently thinking about how desire may have the same etymological root as the word deserve. Maybe all things we desire were meant for us, and everything we want, we actually deserve. If you want something, you are destined to get it. What you seek is seeking you. This, I think, is a nice way to look at Mars: our initiative and passion about getting what we want. Even if it means egoism and aggression sometimes. This is an important counterpart to Venus, because, sometimes, we need to leave behind our good and well-mannered behavior and stop silencing ourselves for the sake of Venusian peace. Sometimes we need to express our passion and desires and go after what we want (and deserve), we need to speak out and be angry about the right thing. An evolved Mars is not about war, but about the protection of the weak. No one wins in a war. An evolved Mars is a hero that fights for something, has a cause, shows chivalry, is active and independent, is driven by bravery, enthusiasm, proves to be assertive and conquers that which he intended to conquer. At the best, the defensive Mars puts his energy into defending his own and the rights of others. He is a courageous leader.

However, before Mars can develop into this very mature expression of his own archetype, he has to grow up. He is the ruler of the newborn baby in the zodiac after all. Aries is the sign that rules the season of spring, of the rebirth of nature and the emergence of bursting life and vitality. He is very innocent and childlike. He has an unaware and naïve quality about him, always showing initiative, playing around and being quite accident-prone.

> *"It may be the wrong decision, but fuck it, it's mine."*
> Mark Z. Danielewski

Much like an excited and fascinated child is attracted to play, the Mars iron is attracted to the Venus magnet. In Greek mythology, Ares and Aphrodite were lovers (and siblings) and Mars (Ares) relates to the energy that conquers, while Venus (Aphrodite) relates to the energy that is being conquered. Mars goes out and fights to achieve something while Venus just leans back, receives, and enjoys. These are the archetypal energetic patterns of yin and yang. Mars is the knight in shining armor that chases his conquest and courts his desired Venus. Venus savors and receives love, presents, and other signs of appreciation and infatuation. If one were to describe the Mars energy in one word it would be "Penetration". Although sexual desire (on an almost animalistic level) is a main theme of Mars, the archetype is also penetrating in many other fields. Austin Coppock once said that, without Venus, Mars would rape his mother. That is why this planet was seen as a "negative" influence in the horoscope – it describes sexual lust or blood lust which can make someone act absolutely irrational and violent. Although, without Mars, we would have no will to even survive and pursue goals, its raging desire and force can be dangerous, too. Mars is actually exalted in Capricorn – his anger is most reasonable and his conquests show the most endurance and stamina in this cardinal earth sign. Capricorn is symbolized by a goat with a fish tail, which is a phallic symbol. So Mars is all about learning not to think with your penis (literal or not) and to not be carried away with a rush of adrenaline that would result in a childish temper tantrum – or worse.

Mars and the sign it is in shows our idea of masculinity. When someone strongly identifies with being male, it shows the type of man he wants to be. It describes the way that person acts when, for example, trying to conquer a romantic or sexual interest or proving his masculinity in any other way. The Mars in our charts is our personal archetypal ideal man.

Therefore, in the case of someone who does not primarily identify as male, Mars is something that they disidentify with and projected onto others –it is the type of man someone is attracted to.

♂ Mars in ♈ Aries

Anger and passion is expressed impulsively and aggressively, dies out as spontaneously as it erupted, ideal of masculinity as being heroic and bossy, a manly man.

♂ Mars in ♉ Taurus

Anger and passion builds up slowly and is expressed stubbornly and with endurance, ideal of masculinity as being reliable and sensual, a tender provider.

♂ Mars in ♊ Gemini

Anger and passion is expressed in a rational way, verbal expressions of rage, flares up quickly, with little harsh feelings left, ideal of masculinity as being intellectual and witty, a clever youth.

♂ Mars in ♋ Cancer

Anger and passion is expressed passive-aggressively and in a sensitive manner, sulky, might evoke sympathy as their weapon, ideal of masculinity as being nurturing and romantic.

♂ Mars in ♌ Leo

Anger and passion is expressed dramatically and theatrically, does not take criticism well, ideal of masculinity as being loud, proud and entertaining.

♂ Mars in ♍ Virgo

Anger and passion is expressed in a composed and

reasonable way, hates losing control, ideal of masculinity as being capable and refined with a clean image.

♂ Mars in ♎ Libra

Anger and passion is expressed with tact and charm, willing to compromise, ideal of masculinity as being elegant and charming with refined tastes.

♂ Mars in ♏ Scorpio

Anger and passion is expressed in extreme ways, holds grudges and can be devious, ideal of masculinity as being intense and mysterious with lots of charisma and passion.

♂ Mars in ♐ Sagittarius

Anger and passion is expressed in a somewhat exaggerated manner, especially in face of injustice, ideal of masculinity as being educated and cosmopolitan, someone who "can show you the world".

♂ Mars in ♑ Capricorn

Anger and passion is expressed reasonably and with endurance, ideal of masculinity as being ambitious and mature, a businessman.

♂ Mars in ♒ Aquarius

Anger and passion is expressed rebelliously and innovatively, ideal of masculinity as being humanitarian and collegial.

♂ **Mars in ♓ Pisces**

Anger and passion is expressed indirectly (either with compassion for others or through manipulation), ideal of masculinity as being empathetic and poetic – an artist or romantic.

♂ Mars in 1ˢᵗ House

Passionate and energetic self-presentation, easily irritated and heated up in matters concerning their identity (and threats to it), comes across as very direct and forceful.

♂ Mars in 2ⁿᵈ House

Passionate and energetic about their possessions and values (fighting to acquire and protect them), easily irritated and heated up when those possessions or values are threatened by others, territorial about their belongings.

♂ Mars in 3ʳᵈ House

Passionate and energetic manner of speech, easily irritated and heated up in conversations, prone to verbal fights or intellectual competition.

♂ Mars in 4ᵗʰ House

Passionate and energetic about their heritage and roots, easily irritated and heated up when their family is attacked, protective about them, independent from an early age, might come from an aggressive home.

♂ Mars in 5ᵗʰ House

Passionate and energetic about their hobbies and sex life, easily irritated and heated up when playing games – very competitive, loves to conquer others and can be very jealous, passionate lover.

♂ Mars in 6th House

Passionate and energetic about daily routines (might enjoy regular workouts), easily irritated and heated up in matters concerning their work, competitive at their workplace, difficulty with team work, workaholic.

♂ Mars in 7th House

Passionate and energetic about relationships (dominating over partner or dominated by partner), easily irritated and heated up in matters concerning their partners or have a partner who is easily irritated, very direct with equals, show initiative in approaching them.

♂ Mars in 8th House

Passionate and energetic about taboos (challenging and being passionate about off-limit topics), easily irritated and heated up in matters concerning intimate bonds with or power over people, high sex drive, destructive.

♂ Mars in 9th House

Passionate and energetic about their worldview, easily irritated and heated up in matters concerning personal ideologies, tend to push their beliefs on others and be aggressive about their ideals.

♂ Mars in 10th House

Passionate and energetic about pursuing goals, easily irritated and heated up in matters concerning their image and reputation, can be successful in a Marsian career (leadership, entrepreneurship, pioneering or athletic work).

♂ Mars in 11th House

Passionate and energetic about one's dreams and visions, easily irritated and heated up in matters concerning their social network, can easily get involved in fights with/of their friends.

♂ Mars in 12th House

Passion and energy are abandoned, not very active, suppression of sexual and aggressive feelings, doesn't like confrontation.

JUPITER

*"Happiness is not a state to arrive at,
but a manner of travelling."*
Margaret Lee Runbeck

The Sanskrit word for *Jupiter* is guru. Jupiter is our inner guru or the part of us that wants to be a guru. It is our quest for wisdom and truth. Jupiter is constantly asking "what's the meaning of this? What's the meaning of life?" – it is all about the big, fundamental questions. This part within us strives for enlightenment and sometimes just for a good conversation about god and the world. Our Jupiter wants to develop a philosophy of life, a personal worldview and their own opinions on religion and politics. Since Jupiter is associated with religion, people with a strong Jupiter in their chart are said to be religious and have a strong faith – this conjures up the image of a devout Christian who prays daily. However, this merely indicates a deep belief, trust and faith in *something* – even if that is atheism or a political ideology.

Jupiter shows what we consider our truth. It is the worldview or ideas that we preach and teach, what we believe is the right thing to believe about god, the world, the universe, society… Often, our personal truth can be seen as the absolute truth, though, and we desperately want everyone to see that we are right.

This is the mentor or priest(ess) archetype – that conscience within each of us that judges themselves and others based on their set of beliefs and morality. This is the part of us which judges what we do from a moral and ideological standpoint and goes "Shame on you!" whenever we or somebody else deviates from our worldview of what is right or true – what is the way to act, live, what to believe. However, since Jupiter is usually quite self-righteous, he judges others more so than himself and can be a big hypocrite.

All these dogmas and all of this bigotry can be taken to unhealthy extents, but a certain sense of morality, belief and righteousness is crucial. Jupiter always asks "What is the meaning of this, how does it fit into the bigger picture?" He believes in some higher, divine order, he believes that life has meaning.

When we trust and believe in the meaning of life, in some higher order and truth, it gives us a lot of confidence. Especially because we think that we follow the *right* religion, the *right* ideology, the *right* worldview, the *right* truth. We think we are good and just, so we are optimistic – surely, we must be rewarded for knowing and following the only truth. Sagittarius is the sign that is ruled by Jupiter and I am a Sagittarius with a Sagittarius Ascendent, and a Jupiter / sun conjunction. I myself am strongly influenced by this archetypal energy and, ironically, this whole book is me preaching my truth and pantheistic worldview. Jupiter does make us feel like we are in an elevated position that justifies us teaching others our wisdom – when, really, the true wisdom of Jupiter is understanding that everyone is a teacher. Everyone has Jupiter in their chart, everyone has something to teach. We mustn't get stuck in a worldview, we must always be open to expanding our consciousness.

If we have faith in something, it makes us confident, whether that faith is religious, spiritual, scientific or ideological. It allows us to think big, to be expansive. Jupiter is linked to generosity, because, where there is trust and faith that there'll always be enough, a sense of abundance, one can easily give. Jupiter is good and generous but this can often come from an arrogant position of "You poor stupid peasants I will be so good and give you some of my riches and wisdom- I have enough of it anyways!"
Jupiter is abundance and luck but can also be the part within ourselves that is too relaxed and pushes their luck. It is the energy that is way too confident, preachy and self-righteous. It has been said that an optimist is someone who sees taking two steps forward and one back as a cha-cha. However, he may never learn the lesson about his set-backs and keep on committing the same mistake, being stuck and too optimistic about it.

I see Jupiter as the chubby Buddha – jovial, wise, abundant, indulgent, enlightened, happy, a deep belly laugh escaping from him, enjoying life, being the carefree guru that he is and never taking anything seriously. Jupiter is connected to our sense of humor, our ability to look at life with a sense of humor, to wink back at the universe and see everything as a divine comedy. When this part within us is overly pronounced, we can have a mentality of "Life is a dance floor and God is the DJ", we will constantly be celebrating. This is the motivational speaker inside your head, the voice that pushes your confidence. The wisdom of this planet is that you are a child of the universe and that it is the most loving and accepting mother and father you could ever imagine. The very fabric of the universe is love, it is what you have been woven from. Therefore, when you – consciously or unconsciously – tell yourself that it is not possible for you to have something, that you don't deserve it, the universe will respond by saying "Then so be it". It does not judge, it gives you what you believe you deserve getting, it gives you what you think you are allowed to ask for. Because you are it. You are the universe. You get what you are willing to give to yourself, what you are open to receiving. Jupiter will tell you not to be humble, to take everything you could possibly get from life. He smiles down at you with his wise and warm grin, puts his hand on your shoulder and says "You deserve it. Treat yourself."

However, Jupiter can very easily take on an excessive quality. Jupiter is the gas giant that blows out of proportion and exaggerates everything it touches. Jupiter is literally and figuratively just hot air. He can throw a lot of inspirational quotes into the room, without actually being wise or enlightened. He will brag about all his riches that are just a façade to his humongous debts. Jupiter simply assumes that he should get anything he wants without having to work for it. Nothing is good enough for Jupiter, the grass is always greener on the other side and the horizon line is constantly receding.

Jupiter wants more and more expansion, more and more abundance, always more, more, more. He has to realize that one is rich to the degree that one can give, that the gift is in the giving. Somebody who is truly rich does not see giving as sacrifice. However, the dark side of Jupiter is his sense of superiority that is connected to one's conviction that the world view one holds is the absolute and only right one, that one is better or above others in one way or another. This turns one into a moral preacher, a guru, a teacher, puts one on a high horse, thinking others have to learn from them. The irony, of course, is that Jupiter rules Sagittarius, the sign of the centaur, which is anatomically destined to always be on a literal high horse.

If we think that we are right and moral and good we can gain a hypocritical holier-than-thou attitude. Hypocritical because, without Saturn, the ideals and morality of Jupiter will lack integrity and responsibility – practical application. This feeling of being "God's favorite", thinking we have this divine spark within us that makes us special, above mere mortals. This, too, is shown in the symbol of the centaur: half horse, half man – above the animal nature, called for something higher.

Jupiter is lazy yet never content with the best, full of himself, thinks that everything should be served on a silver platter for him, yet he never moves a finger himself – like a god being fed with grapes, spitting them out because they weren't sweet enough for him.

This exaggeration, overdoing, overextending of oneself is very typical of this archetype. He is lucky, but he pushes his luck. He is confident in himself but also very self-righteous, unable to take any criticism – he is divinely superior, after all.

This sense of spiritual or religious purpose and this faith in meaning and magic is an important part in our horoscopes. I probably made it sound like Jupiter is primarily bad. However, the fact that Jupiter brings luck, abundance, confidence and optimism is often so over pronounced that I wanted to point out the duality that is inherent in every archetype.

Rising above our animal nature is not just a haughty, self-absorbed attitude. It also shows our actual ability of gaining wisdom and educating ourselves. Jupiter is known as the "higher mind", "higher intellect" or "higher education". Its archetype corresponds to that of the wanderer, the explorer, the academic, the seeker of wisdom, the religious pilgrim, the vagabond. We experience a shift in perspective on the world and ourselves by travelling and educating ourselves, collecting both experiences and knowledge through travel within and without, meeting other cultures and people, seeing the world through the eyes of somebody else when reading a book. All these things expand our horizons and our consciousness. Universities, libraries, sanctuaries, churches – these are the places that the spirit of Jupiter resides in.

The ultimate wisdom of Jupiter is that horizons recede when we come closer to them - the earth is round after all. So there is no destination, just an everlasting journey. When we realize this and stop arrogantly claiming we know the absolute and only truth we become spiritual and move into the realm of Neptune which has no boundaries doesn't even see a horizon line.

To understand that education is a journey without a destination of "Now I know everything", to understand that your intellectual and spiritual horizons will always keep receding is to become truly open-minded. The world will turn into an academic and ideological playground.

Everyone can teach you something. You might not like being taught, but everyone has in them a teacher and mentor – their natal Jupiter.

Everyone has a unique perspective on the universe. Everyone's perspective is "right", in the sense that it is their personal truth.

In our quest for the truth we might never arrive, but that does not stop the optimistic spirit of Jupiter, that is always ready for adventure. The Sagittarius archer shoots his arrow at the horizon, aiming for wisdom, experience, knowledge. "What is out there? What is the meaning of everything?" It is the vision of the possibility to someday be enlightened that keeps Jupiter going – to one day be able to pass on the wisdom.

> *"Life has no meaning. Each of us has meaning and we bring it to life. It is a waste to be asking the question when you are the answer."*
> Joseph Campbell

While on the pursuit of happiness, it is important to focus on the journey rather than the destination. What is the

destination you're chasing, that thing that, once you reach it, finally allows you to be happy? "Once I'm in a relationship, I will be happy!"
'Relationship' can be replaced by 'high paying job' or whatever else your little heart desires.
The point is, many of us are constantly waiting to arrive somewhere and *once* we are there – and only then – can we really be happy. What is the destination you are chasing? A happy family? Retirement?
And then what? I don't think we will ever fully arrive, thinking "That is it. Nothing needs to be added or changed ever."
That is a thought for your death bed.
For now, don't worry about arriving anywhere. I hate to be the embodiment of the Jupiter archetype (or, actually – I don't. It's pretty neat being this optimistic), but: *Enjoy the journey.*
This is such a cliché, but it's true. The past does not exist, the future does not exist and some alternate reality fantasy world does not exist either (although I like to believe it does), all we ever have is the now. This exact now. As you are reading this. This is your life. What you choose to do with it. Thank you, by the way, for choosing to read my book. If we only ever chase a destination because we believe it means happiness, we can just cut out the middle man and choose happiness in the now. If that means painting, listening to music, calling a friend – do that! If it means closing this book – by all means, do that!
If all you take from this book is that you only ever have the now, so you should make a happy journey, that is enough.

♃ Jupiter in 1st House

Faith and trust in self, philosophy of life built around identity (á la "Life is about creating yourself"), confident about one's abilities, this placement makes one come across as very confident, jovial and generous.

♃ Jupiter in 2nd House

Faith and trust in possessions, philosophy of life built around financial and material wealth, confident about one's resources, this placement makes one a big spender, because one believes that there will always be enough.

♃ Jupiter in 3rd House

Faith and trust in one's knowledge, philosophy of life built around facts, confident about one's ideas and opinions, this placement makes one talk a lot and exaggerate when speaking.

♃ Jupiter in 4th House

Faith and trust in one's roots, philosophy of life built around what they have been taught in their early upbringing (adopts the parents' worldviews), confident about being popular/"the best" in one's family, this placement makes one proud of one's heritage.

♃ Jupiter in 5th House

Faith and trust in one's creative abilities, philosophy of life built around "live, love, laugh", confident about one's loveableness, this placement makes one (be able to) count on one's luck and the favors of others.

♃ Jupiter in 6th House

Faith and trust in one's ability to cope with daily tasks, philosophy of life built around everyday routine, confident at work, this placement makes one successful at their job.

♃ Jupiter in 7th House

Faith and trust in others, philosophy of life built around relationships and partnerships, confident about one's ability to get along with and be popular with others, this placement makes one a sociable people-person.

♃ Jupiter in 8th House

Faith and trust in one's emotional depths, philosophy of life built around experiences of transformation, confident about one's personal power (which might be abused), this placement makes one keep their pride and confidence even in the most challenging life phases.

♃ Jupiter in 9th House

Faith and trust in one's righteousness and worldview, philosophy of life built around religions or ideologies, confident about their wisdom, this placement makes one very devoted to and preachy about their beliefs.

♃ Jupiter in 10th House

Faith and trust in one's life path, philosophy of life built around climbing the ladder of success, confident about one's career, this placement can indicate fame or a career in teaching.

♃ Jupiter in 11th House

Faith and trust in humanity, philosophy of life built around contributing to society, confident about being a good friend, this placement makes one popular or have a network of supporters and benefactors.

♃ Jupiter in 12th House

Faith and trust in spirituality, philosophy of life built around sacrifice, confident about one's ability to be alone, this placement makes one find joy in solitude and selflessness.

SATURN

*"Experience: that most brutal of teachers.
But you learn, my God do you learn."*
C.S. Lewis

Saturn is the last visible planet in the solar system; for thousands of years it was believed to be the outermost planet and was called the "Dweller at the Threshold". Now we know there's also Uranus, Neptune and Pluto, but for the majority of human history, Saturn was the line between the visible and the unknown – it served as a boundary. Even now, Saturn is still associated with psychological boundaries. It describes our fears that make us stick to what we know. Saturn restricts and holds us back, it shows our blockages. Saturn wants to contain, to create clear structures and to define. To define is to limit. This is why Saturn, in ancient and medieval astrology, was feared and equivalent to the Old Testament God who would punish you if you crossed any boundaries and did anything that did not match your duties and responsibilities. Saturn was associated with harvest in Roman mythology, it is also tied to what we can reap after hard work. It pretty much follows the parenting method of "punishment and reward".

In this sense, Saturn is also often associated with Karma and has been called "The Lord of Karma"; punishing and rewarding the things you do with equal payoff. This planet is exalted in the sign of Libra, the sign of the scales; equality. Saturn will always be fair. He is the judge who will give you exactly what you deserve. He does not simply act on whims; what goes around is exactly what will come around. Saturn is very literal and very fair.

Saturn being within us shows that we are our own judge. Court is a mental place. Saturn is associated with Satanism, which is why Satan is portrayed with the horns and legs of a goat; Capricorn. Hell is not a physical place – it is our bad conscience – it is us judging ourselves and our lives – most profoundly at an old age.

We are our own karma. Consequently, Saturn could be described as that part within us that creates personal boundaries and responsibilities and punishes themselves for either crossing them or not sticking to them. We cage ourselves. The way we initially adopt this is through socialization. We are born fearless and assuming unconditional love and abundance. Saturn is the second social planet next to Jupiter and describes the restrictions, doubts and fears we adopted through figures of authority, often the father, during socialization. Saturn represents the strict parent that told us to fit in and made us internalize feelings of insecurity. This planet represents authority figures and how we perceive(d) them. This is usually the father but sometimes the mother or teachers or peers – anyone we gave or still give the power to decide over what we do and who we are. Saturn teaches us to fit in and to restrict and discipline ourselves to be functioning members of society. Saturn makes you adjust out of fear of being different and wrong and unacceptable. He is the victim of authority. The victim and follower of what people tell him to be. We start judging ourselves for not doing well enough. The discouraging voices we received from our environment transform into inner voices and imprint themselves on our psyche. They are expressed in fear, insecurity and a feeling of lack in whichever house it is in.

Saturn does not represent a purely bad influence, though. It takes time for this planet to mature, but when it does, it will realize its authority and make you gain the power to decide what and who you want to be in the area of life it controls. This planet will transform into a force of self-sufficiency, independence and the urge to work hard for the goals and standards they have set for themselves. A mature Saturn is not controlled by other people's dictations and expectations; it is its very own authority. So, with Saturn, we have to go through a sort of developmental process. He urges us to (re)claim our own authority, to take on the responsibility of deciding who to be and what to do, to concentrate on ambition rather than fear, on what we have to offer (can be a master or authority in), rather than on what we lack.

The thing is that we can only master something through practice – by doing it again and again – but we are also especially scared of this area of life. It's like we're constantly being tested. At the same time, we have to pretend we're not struggling, to be acceptable and presentable publically and socially. We pretend we're just as capable and confident as everyone else, when we are anything but that. The truth is, we are (and especially feel like) complete losers wherever Saturn is placed.

Saturn will never simply let you resign though. When you say "I don't want to struggle anymore, or pretend to know what I'm doing!", Saturn says "put on your big girl panties and deal with it." He does not allow excuses or shortcuts and will always pull you back down onto the ground of the harsh facts of reality. Saturn wants you to grow up, suck it up, and stop being a baby.

Saturn has been called our Achilles' heel, since it shows our biggest insecurity and weakness, where we are most vulnerable and fearful. Because we are so insecure about this part of us, it makes us a bit awkward in whatever field is indicated by the house placement. Saturn makes us feel like everyone else is far ahead of us in that area of life and like we're incapable, stumbling behind clumsily. We have to experience more hardships and more hard lessons than others in this area. It's like Saturn said "You! You are special! I know you can handle this, so I will make you go through especially much, just so you can develop and grow more than anyone else. It will be hard but I trust that you can make it, that you will get through your awkward stage and get out the other end being an absolute master of this area of life!" When we feel incapable of doing something as well as everyone else, maybe that means we have to learn to do it *our way* instead! Trust yourself to know how you should do it. Maybe doing it differently is a gift, after all, when you learn to recognize it.

Wherever Saturn is placed, we will have to develop from fear, restriction, limitation, conformity, humility and pessimism to authority, responsibility, control, respect, wisdom and ambition. We go from the one to the other by experiencing Saturnian lessons of maturation.

Saturn is like an old mean man forcing us to climb a huge, steep mountain. We're struggling, wondering "What's the point? Why are you making me go through this?" But when we make it – we're at the peak, we can look down at the whole path we've taken, we see the whole world at our feet, tiny from up here - we suddenly understand – we see the structure of everything – from up here, everything makes sense, all the struggle. The struggle and the people that caused your struggle are your Saturnian mentors. Looking back, you will see the face of Saturn in every person that has disrespected you and in every situation that got you down on your knees (Saturn rules the knees). And then you get the lesson – because now, the view is breathtaking. From up here, we can say: "It was all worth it, because now I am here. The struggle was necessary. Without it, I would not have gained wisdom." It also makes us develop a lot of respect for ourselves. We can look down at the steep path with all the rocks in our way and say: "I made it up here. I guess I am pretty tough. I am both strong and wise through my experiences and struggles. That's why I deserve respect and am an authority!"

Where Saturn falls into your chart, you will experience lack and struggle. Like you're looking at everyone else hanging out at the lake sipping juice and you're being forced to climb this mountain at the foot of the lake. "Why can't I join them? I don't want to struggle; I just want to be like them!" But when you've made it up the mountain, you'll know why it was good to not be with them. Saturn turns slaves into masters and beggars into rich men. We all have one area of life in which we are slaves and beggars – where we feel like we have to follow other's authority and struggle to "feel rich". If we resist the challenge, don't listen to Saturn forcing us up the mountain, we will just keep on sitting on a dry rock looking down at others sipping juice at the lake. If we surrender to Saturn's tough lessons, we will reach the top.

Capricorn is the sign ruled by Saturn, that's why they're represented by the goat – they can climb the steepest mountains with ease.

Saturn is the planet of law and order, it rules police and other types of law enforcement. It wants to conserve structures that have been build, organize their world and make everything work out according to set rules. Saturn is the conserver. He is conservative. Eyes set firmly on top of the mountain, he does not like to stray from the path.

The Saturn glyph consists of the *Crescent of Soul* with the *Cross of Matter* on top of it. Matter over soul. Because Saturn shows restrictions in general, it rules the two things that restrict us humans the most – time and space – the material plane, the three-dimensional reality. In mythology, Saturn is also known as Chronos, God of Time. Saturn is the celestial hourglass; it reminds us of our restrictions. It rules time and any other boundaries. Chronos, the time keeper, reminds us of the lack of time – basically the lack of everything – and makes us feel like there is never enough and like we are never enough, it pressures us, because it makes us feel there's not enough time for us to do what we want to do.

Saturn also rules lead, the dense and heavy metal. Saturn drags and slows you down, it can make you feel like the weight of the whole world is on your shoulders. In medical astrology, it rules our bones and skin – our physical boundary, but also "our backbone". According to spiritual teacher Teal Swan, there is a problem with osteoporosis in areas of the world where there is a problem with authority. According to her, if you don't trust you're the authority of your own life, it will weaken your bones. A strong Saturn says "I'm the only one who thinks for me!", but a weak Saturn will doubt their ability to be safe in the world, to maintain themselves. It does not trust its ability to think for itself, it constantly resists outside control, is tight and rigid, does not trust in security. Teal says that resistant people are a match to acidic things (acid is ruled by Saturn), such as acidic people and foods, which will, in the end, make them have weak bones – a physical manifestation of the weak psychological Saturn.

Saturn also rules teeth. We have to chew and bite our way through the Saturnian lessons slowly and thoroughly to be able to digest them properly. Old patterns come up again and again until we *really* get the lesson. Like a ruminating cow. It seems to throw us back into the same issue again and again, the pattern keeps resurfacing.

When we are about fourteen years old, Saturn will have

travelled 180° since the moment of our birth and create an opposition to our natal Saturn. This is the time of puberty and quite literally the point in our lives where we feel the highest degree of opposition towards authority, specifically our parents or teachers. When we reach the age of about twenty-eight to thirty years, we experience our Saturn return – this is when Saturn is back at the place of the zodiac it was in during our birth, a cycle is completed, the planet has travelled a whole 360°. This is the point in our lives when we realize how old we have become, when we feel the burden of being a real grown up adult. Most people really dread turning thirty because of this. The next Saturn opposition, the next opposition to authority and maturity, happens at the age of about forty-five, the midlife crisis, the rebellion against old age, the feeling of having missed out on something, having been restricted too much – by yourself or others.

In spite of all the challenges it poses for us, I've learned to love Saturn the way I do Pluto – the "malefics" bring us the most growth. Saturn is the Old Mercury. It is the knowledge we gain with experience. Chronos rules time so we do need to reach a certain age to truly get what the Saturnian lessons and tests have taught us (since I've not been through my Saturn return yet I don't claim to have gained absolute wisdom when it comes to this).

Being the ruler of time and structure, Saturn helps us to manage our time and be productive. Whenever we go through a major Saturn transit, we might feel like our experiences drag on and on, like time stretches like chewing gum. Again, Saturn *really* wants you to get his lesson. "Do it properly, take your time!" he says.

Since this is the last visible planet it has been called "the final boss", which I think is really cool; it is the last challenge that will free you, explode your boundaries and limitations. However, I'm not sure that, after the discovery of the modern planets, this still holds true. Uranus, Neptune and Pluto are like the later added bonus levels, with Pluto being the true final challenge.

Saturn is not as serious as people sometimes think he is, he does have a dry and dark sense of humor that is a bit hard to detect. He does rule boundaries, but there are very important and healthy boundaries; saying "no" when we mean "no" and saying "yes" when we mean "yes" is a sign of healthy boundaries and personal integrity. To draw lines, having personal boundaries, defining how people can treat you and what is not okay is a strength of Saturn. He also makes you develop your own set of values and makes you stick to them with integrity, rather than doing your duty simply because others tell you to.

Saturn always boils down to fear and insecurity and it can always be transformed and exalted into authority and wisdom. Although these seem like contradicting energies, they're actually two sides of the same coin; absence of authority and presence of it are the same energy in different states. Whether you give it up or claim it is your decision and in your personal power. You will also realize that somebody else having authority does not equal a lack of it in yourself. We don't have to steal it off of others, there's an infinite abundance of it.

While Saturn was transiting my sun, I wrote into my journal: *Respect has to be demanded. Authority is not given to you, you rise up to it.* It was then that I realized that you shouldn't wait for a shift outside of you – the gods are literally within you and the exterior world is merely a reflection, a mirror, to the interior one. You, at any moment in your personal development, can decide to rise up to a position of influence, respect and authority. It's like you're going "Wait a minute – when and why did I give the power to judge my deserving of respect and authority away to others?" The whole nature of Saturn is about rising up to the wisdom that the master and teacher is *inside* of you – so you are the only one who can decide what you deserve! You have to reach a point where you go "Okay – no more. This can't go on! I will be my only authority from now on, do whatever I want and express myself freely." The only way to really commit to this is by feeling the burden of being restricted in the first place. Only when we struggle we desire to become better, to improve. Only when we feel we lack, we work on ourselves.

Saturn wants us to stop making excuses. It's very easy to say something like "Well, they're not going to take me seriously anyways" or "But *they* have the control, not me!" Saturn challenges escapism – it wants us to really take responsibility for our own situation. Once you do, you don't have to prove anything to anyone anymore, because you know yourself! You will not run to defenses, because others' opinions don't control you or let you shiver in fear anymore. That extent of inherent self-trust and self-respect is what develops through Saturn and his tests, lessons and restrictions. Saturn is very self-sufficient so it teaches you that, rather than begging for respect and acceptance from others, you should give it to yourself first. And then they will follow. Trust and respect yourself enough to keep on track of the climb of your own mountain, not someone else's. I have a quote hanging over my work space which reads "It's better to be at the bottom of the ladder you want to climb than to be on the top of one you don't" which captures the Saturnian wisdom perfectly.

Saturn rules business and it is both the anchor that gives you a reality check but also the weight that drags you down and turns you into the pessimistic, workaholic party pooper. The importance is to find the Libran balance.

♄ Saturn in 1st House

Fearful and conforming personality, is insecure about who they are and seeks approval for their identity, clumsy self-expression, seeks respect and can develop a role of authority. This makes one be mature and well put-together but very judgmental about themselves. They exude an air of authority and naturally take on responsibility. Can be too serious and pessimistic in their approach to life.

♄ Saturn in 2nd House

Fearful about possessions (losing them or not having enough), conforms to other people's sets of values, has low self-worth and seeks approval from others to feel worthy. Greedy at worst and frugal at best. Either amount possessions to feel secure or have to learn to find security within themselves. Minimalists.

♄ Saturn in 3rd House

Fearful about expressing themselves, might not talk much and conforms to other people's opinions and thoughts, insecure about their knowledge, scared that they are or sound stupid when they speak, clumsy conversationalist, can develop into an impactful speaker whose opinions and knowledge are respected.

♄ Saturn in 4th House

Fearful and conforming at home, is insecure when it comes to their emotional expression and seeks approval from their family, clumsy at nurturing and being nurtured, might have constant feelings of slight anxiety, which imprinted themselves onto their psyche in a strict household.

♄ Saturn in 5th House

Fearful about showing themselves off, because they fear they aren't lovable, is insecure when it comes to seeking fun and pleasure and seeks approval from others for this – feel they need permission to enjoy themselves. Clumsy at giving or receiving love. Learns to manage work and play and to have fun in a responsible way.

♄ Saturn in 6th House

Fearful and conforming in their job, is insecure when it comes to their ability to serve others and seeks approval from others when it comes to their ability to do what is asked of them, clumsy at organizing and fulfilling tasks, seeks respect and can develop into an authority in their work and amongst co-workers.

♄ Saturn in 7th House

Fearful and conforming in relationships, is insecure when it comes to romance and seeks approval from others in general, clumsy at relating to others, scared of being judged, seeks respect and can develop into an authority in teamwork and interpersonal contact in general. These individuals might project a lot of their own inhibiting qualities onto others, rather than being aware of them within themselves.

♄ Saturn in 8th House

Scared of intimacy, is insecure when it comes to emotional

vulnerability and letting go of control, clumsy at opening up. Emotional rigidity, scared of people abusing them and therefore very guarded. Doesn't let their walls down easily. By overcoming the fear of crisis and personal transformation, they can gain emotional security and authority over their vulnerability.

♄ Saturn in 9th House

Fearful and conforming in their worldview, is insecure when it comes to beliefs and seeks approval from others in their ideology, seeks respect and can develop into an authority in teaching. Growing up, a religion, ideology or worldview was imposed on them that they now fear to question. Insecure about their own beliefs and philosophies.

♄ Saturn in 10th House

Fearful and conforming in their career, is insecure when it comes to their image and reputation, clumsy in the public eye, seeks respect and can develop into an authority in their worldly achievements and the respect they receive. Might feel pressured to follow the footsteps of a parent, because it shows tradition in the career.

♄ Saturn in 11th House

Fearful of social groups, is insecure when it comes to friends and peers and seeks approval from them, clumsy at networking, seeks respect and can develop into an authority in their group of friends and acquaintances – a reliable and respected person in their social network. Might fear the future and doesn't allow themselves to dream big.

♄ Saturn in 12th House

Fears chaos and the unknown, disciplines themselves to not "lose themselves", is insecure when it comes to escapism and seeks approval or permission for isolating themselves and retreating from time to time, clumsy at spiritual practices, will not allow themselves to give in to their unconscious depths and illogical anxieties but will have to master this part of themselves.

URANUS

"It is the first responsibility of every citizen to question authority."
Benjamin Franklin

The movie *Into the Wild* tells the true story of Christopher McCandless, a Uranus-dominant Aquarius. He burns all his belongings in an act of rebellion and runs away from home to live in the wilderness. At the end (spoiler!), he dies from eating a poisoned plant and his last realization is that "Happiness is only real when shared", while dying alone in the middle of nowhere, miles away from civilization. Having this archetype be quite strong in my own birth chart as well, I highly relate to the dichotomy of this. On the one hand, you feel alienated and want to rebel, but on the other hand, there is this realization that we exist and find happiness and live out our purpose not only on our own, but within a group of people. We are all connected, we are social beings and don't live in isolation. What we do has an effect on everyone around us, it's an intricate network. The Uranus archetype is both too caught up within themselves but also learns to realize their duty of serving all of humanity; that what we do affects the whole. The best term to associate this with is probably "collective consciousness".

Since Uranus is quite detached and futuristic, it creates the sort of connection that is buzzing and electric – the kind you can feel at a protest, at a round-table, and sometimes in social media. Uranus is a transpersonal planet that makes you feel like a part of something bigger, like all of humanity is a family. When networks take on this gigantic a scope, one can feel detached, the intimacy is lost – although everyone is connected, the relationships are platonic and a means to an end, rather than simply a celebration of togetherness (like Venus).

Uranus' ruling sign Aquarius is often mistaken for a water sign, even though it actually is an air sign. The symbol of the water bearer is representative of humanitarianism. Water is the source of life and the stereotypical Aquarius can have a bit of a God complex and feel like a savior that is here to liberate and enlighten humanity. Richard Tarnas first illustrated the similarities between the archetype of Uranus and the Greek myth of Prometheus. The latter was the one who stole the fire from the gods to give it to man. Symbolically, the giving of water (Aquarius) or fire (Prometheus) to man has similar implications – it empowers the crowds. Uranus is the counterpart to authority and represents anarchy and rebellion. The archetype of the mad scientist comes out in the story of Prometheus as well, when he built man from mud – another rebellious act that mocked the power of the Olympian Gods.

Uranus represents genius, that innovative part within us that sparks progress, thinks differently, and may cause a quantum leap. The waves of the Aquarius symbol represent this constant progress of a humankind that is dreaming of a utopian society. The only way to cause innovation is to be different and Uranus paints the picture of an alien species coming down on earth to provide futuristic scientific tools and ideas. Some conspiracy theorists say that Jesus was an alien hybrid and that the Egyptian pyramids were built with the help of aliens, but that's a whole other topic.

In my sociology lecture about social norms, innovation was defined as the acceptance of a society's goals and ideals with a simultaneous rejection of its legitimate means of achieving them. So, innovation is pretty much all about rebellious experimentation, finding new ways of doing something by swimming against the current.
Karl Marx, the infamous socialist, just so happens to have a strong Uranus in his horoscope, the planet of innovation and equality. Uranus is the planet that indicates rebellion in a person's horoscope and it is also really strong in the horoscope of James Dean, the epitome of the rebel figure. Next time you're reading a horoscope and Uranus is mentioned, you can expect sudden changes, coincidences and surprises!
Talking about sudden changes: Uranus was accidentally found by William Herschel and was the first modern planet to be discovered! There's even more coincidences and weird synchronicities: The discovery was in 1781, the time of the French Revolution and other important shifts in the social and political landscape of Europe. And, since Uranus is the planet of rebellion, individuality, anarchy and changes, this planet's motto might very well be "Liberté,

Égalité, Fraternité".

Uranus deals with the duality of oppression and liberation in our charts, he is always striving for autonomy and refuses to bend under authority. This, however, can turn Uranus into a "rebel without a cause" type – rather than focusing on revolutions that bring about positive changes, he might keep on rebelling against the establishment for the pure sake of rebelling. Wherever Uranus is placed in our charts, we need to realize that true liberation means that the thing you were rebelling against no longer controls you, your actions and your choices. The house that Uranus is placed in is that area of life where we feel most caged in and therefore tend to rebel the most.

Uranus reminds me of the story of the caged bird who is desperately trying to escape, but, once its cage is opened, just stays in it. The band Foster The People have a lot of very Uranian lyrics (their singer has an Aquarius moon), one of my favorites being from the song *Waste*: "You know it's funny how freedom can make us feel contained / Yeah when the muscles in our legs aren't used to all the walking". We need contrast first to be able to appreciate our freedom and often only being stuck and caged in makes us want to break out. If one is given complete freedom to do what they want to do, be who they want to be, and go where they want to go, they will usually be very obedient, because they don't dread the authorities and there is nothing to rebel against. That is also why, maybe paradoxically, anarchy is not a chaotic system, and the parenting method of laisser-faire (letting kids do what they want) creates disciplined children. To take the paradox of Uranus even further, he can often be the same thing that he hates – a fascist. Although Uranus is a revolutionary and fights for freedom, he is just as controlling in his cause as the authorities that he opposes – and turns into a domineering authority himself in the process. This is similar to the problem of communism – forced freedom is a paradox and equality is not always equal. Aquarius is a fixed sign, after all, so this archetype is very stubborn and can forget themselves and the bigger picture in the act of rebellion.

In the pursuit of freedom, Uranus does not fear extreme and radical change. There are no compromises when it comes to ultimate liberation. The more contrast Uranus experiences through Saturnian restrictions and limitations, the stronger the urge for change builds up and eventually erupts. These rebellious thoughts brood for a long time until they suddenly burst out. Uranus always does the unexpected, goes against the norms and mainstream. Much like the trickster Mercury, he will surprise you. Uranus represents that which is unconventional and crazy. He might be seen as a fool, because he is so eccentric and his ideas are so far ahead of his own time, so the genius is bound to be misunderstood. He is the underdog that feels alienated from the rest of society, yet feels deeply connected to humanity. The eternal struggle of Uranus is his hate of rules and systems – he much prefers chaos and will choose to do something completely unexpected and outrageous just to shake it up a little bit and loosen the restraints and the level of seriousness. He loves the shock factor, because he wants to prove his freedom from the rules. Uranus will do something completely weird purely to prove that he isn't stuck in conformity, like Natalie Portman's manic pixie dream girl character in the movie *Garden State* in which she says: "When I feel unoriginal I make a noise or movement no one has ever done before so I can feel unique again." She wants to create "a completely original moment in history". Much like her, Uranus thinks without a box.

We are now in the Age of Aquarius, the so-called "New Age". Besides a progress in technology and a digital, global connection of humanity, we are also moving towards a humanity that is open to being different (spiritual junkies, hipsters,...) and conscious of social justice and equality. A lot of us are free, allowed to vote in democracies, able to go "from rags to riches", live the American Dream. We are highly unaware of how recently we have gained all these opportunities and privileges and of how rare they still are, so we might not make a great use of them. We are the birds sitting in their open cages.

Those of us who aren't Uranus dominant can often subconsciously feel like they aren't allowed to drastically and suddenly change something about themselves or their lives. Hereby, Uranus grants you permission to shock people. To be outrageously unpredictable. If you feel like doing something completely weird and out of the ordinary, just do it. You are allowed to change and you don't need anybody's permission but your own. The only way to find true freedom is to give it to yourself. No matter the external circumstances, we are only ever truly locked up or liberated in our heads to the extent that we allow ourselves to change and be different every second. You don't have to keep being who other people believe you to be just to make them feel secure. Create some chaos. Break some rules. But most importantly: do it because it's liberating, not because you feel stuck. Do it out of a "yes" to freedom, not out of a "no" to restraint. Don't be a rebel without a cause.

♅ Uranus in 1st House

Seeks liberation as an individual (hates to be pigeon-holed), sudden and unpredictable changes in how they present themselves (the role they take in or their physical appearance), unconventional way of seeing the world, eccentric and rebellious, can often feel alienated.

♅ Uranus in 2nd House

Seeks financial freedom, sudden and unpredictable gain or loss of money, unconventional ways of making and spending money, unconventional values, may have unusual talents or be an inventor, may collect unusual things.

♅ Uranus in 3rd House

Seeks freedom of thought, sudden ideas and insights, almost genius, unconventional thinker, original, learns best on their own terms (autodidactic), dislikes the educational system and can feel alienated at school and from (possible) siblings, can't sit still.

♅ Uranus in 4th House

Seeks liberation from their domestic heritage (most of all the parents), sudden and unpredictable changes of residence, unconventional family (patchwork families, families of choice rather than blood relation, etc), feels alienated from family, often there is parental divorce and lots of moving around at an early age, a vagabond without roots.

♅ Uranus in 5th House

Seeks freedom in romance (may never commit deeply), original in creative endeavors, life could suddenly change for the better or the worse through gambling, unconventional and unique ways of expressing themselves creatively, gives their children freedom (laisser-faire approach), unusual hobbies or interests.

♅ Uranus in 6th House

Seeks liberation from traditional 9-5 jobs, sudden and unpredictable changes in occupation or daily routine, unconventional work (science and self-employment are common), humanitarian (feels responsible to serve the progress and liberation of humanity), not very reliable or organized.

♅ Uranus in 7th House

Seeks freedom in relationships (ones that are more like friendships; may even enjoy open relationships or polyamorie), sudden and unpredictable beginnings and endings of relationships, may have unconventional or eccentric partners, hates being caged in by their partners and wants to remain independent from others.

♅ Uranus in 8th House

Seeks liberation from their own intense emotions and drives, sudden and unpredictable personal transformations or inheritances, unconventional or experimental sex life, may have a weird fetish, makes sex independent from partnerships, psychic intuition.

♅ Uranus in 9th House

Seeks liberation from the worldview they were raised with, sudden and unpredictable changes in their higher education, unconventional beliefs (doesn't subscribe to strict rules and dogmas), drawn to travel to weird, exotic places, may study a science or metaphysical subject.

♅ Uranus in 10th House

Seeks liberation in their career, sudden and unpredictable changes in career and/or status, image and reputation as being unconventional, eccentric, or humanitarian, may work in science or technology or be self-employed, dislikes authority and is known as being unauthoritarian.

♅ Uranus in 11th House

Seeks liberation in groups (friends may be weird or rebellious, may be part of an organization promoting change), sudden and unpredictable changes in one's goals and vision for the future (often caused by meeting a group of people with those aspirations), may have unconventional or very progressive visions for the future.

♅ Uranus in 12th House

Seeks liberation through escapism (may only experience freedom in seclusion or by "fleeing" reality), sudden and unpredictable flashes of intuition (may be clairvoyant, ideas often come to them in symbols and dreams), weird dreams which may predict the future and unconventional sleep cycles (may have insomnia or sleep during the day).

NEPTUNE

"Everything you can imagine is real."
Pablo Picasso

Poseidon is the Greek Neptune, the god of the sea. Neptune goes beyond the freedom of Uranus by not only freeing us from mental and physical restraints, but also having a spiritual quality about it. Spiritual freedom means a transcendence of the natural and normal world, as Neptune is supernatural and paranormal. Since this planet is even farther away from the sun than Uranus, it describes an even broader, more subtle and less tangible psychological theme. One that dissolutes the physical realm and turns it into a hazy, blurry ocean of symbols, fantasy and magic. Much like the actual ocean, Neptune is formless and vast. Since it is so indefinite and beyond a three-dimensional reality, Neptune is also associated with death and the afterlife.

Neptune puts us in a trance, in an illusory realm where all Saturnian reality and time-keeping is lost – it's a fantastic blur. Neptune is boundless – it seamlessly flows into everything else. At times, when caught up in Neptunian daydreams and other forms of escapism, we might feel like we're at the bottom of an ocean, the water building a barrier between us and the solid, real world, where the sane people reside.

Whenever we hum the tune of Neptune, we exchange reality for whatever fantasy we want to see. In the house Neptune is in, we might wear rose-tinted glasses and we don't see things for what they really are, we romanticize them. This illusion can, at worst, take over someone's entire life, leaving them being completely deceived about what is real. Neptune will always gladly manipulate the facts and live in an illusion as long as it makes life more easy and enjoyable.

This need for illusion is expressed collectively in the glamorous world of Hollywood and the tabloids. Although the mystery of celebrities as inhuman gods and goddesses has been wearing off, people are now creating their very own illusions on social media. Whether it be a Marilyn Monroe from the classic Hollywood era or the newest YouTube star vlogging their red carpet attendances– when a glamour is cast over something, it is deceiving and not what it seems. Neptune always keeps us from seeing the whole truth and, somehow, people are okay with that. They are obsessed with gossip, glamour and making the world appear more magical than it is and making humans appear as something beyond the human. Neptune will always keep us from accepting that people are just people and life is pretty simple and meaningless. Neptune would rather be deceived and live in a naïve and gullible state than come down to the boring ground of reality.

Since Neptune represents everything that exceeds the physical realm, it also deals with the astral plane and the collective unconscious, the world of dreams, fantasy, and imagination. The dissolution of boundaries also creates a unity with others. To know that we are all one fosters true compassion. Neptune rules the feet, reminding us of how important it is to walk in other people's shoes in order to really understand them. Neptune holds the wisdom that everyone who has ever victimized you was once a victim themselves and that everyone who has ever abused you was once abused, too. Because it makes you see and understand the suffering of the whole world and have empathy for that, Neptune gives you a "turn the other cheek" approach. Being so forgiving, it stands for universal love and the healing that takes place through unconditional acceptance.

On the flipside of that, there is naivety. When the boundaries between you and others are dissolute, there is a blind trust, a complete openness to victimization and abuse. People with strong Neptune influences have so much empathy and trust that they can easily be deceived or taken advantage of. These Neptunians are also very often empaths, meaning that they feel whatever somebody else is feeling as their own feelings. Even on the emotional level, there is a loss of boundaries.

Being so receptive and finely tuned, they can also receive information from higher planes of being. Neptunians are often spiritual, sometimes even psychic, but all of them can trust their guts, because their intuition is really strong. Neptune is so in touch with everything, that it loses connection with the 3D-here-and-now-reality, wandering through life unconsciously, daydreaming. Neptune blurs the boundaries between the conscious, subconscious and collective unconscious, making us see the symbols and illusions from our dreams in our waking life. Since Poseidon rules the ocean, this planet can make us feel as if immersed in a sea of imagination, dreams, and the unconscious. Neptune rules the sign Pisces and, like a fish, people of this sign live as if immersed in the waters of the whole world's emotions, flowing down a stream, passive, and without resistance. Wherever Neptune is placed in our charts we tend to let things unfold rather than taking focused action. Like water, we take the path of least resistance, quite literally "going with the flow". This type of surrender to life makes the Neptune archetype be associated with hippies, drifters, free souls, artists, and even drug addicts. Pisces is a mutable water sign, flowing around any object and fitting in any container. At best, Pisces and Neptune influences make you let the divine take the lead, but at worst – you simply become a sluggish and directionless loser. Like water, there is no resistance. Although this could be interpreted as weakness, by not coming across any defenses, you are not given a place to attack either– like a bullet shooting through water. Neptune lives by the strategy of triumphing over your enemies by making them your friends.

Neptune makes us feel lost, makes us wait to be found. Feeling both cut off from reality but also deeply connected to everything and everyone, the theme of Neptune is that of isolation and unity. In solitude, we can become one with the divine. The realm of Neptune is one of constant wonder and magic, where opposites are the same and paradoxes make sense. As if on drugs, it makes us see the world from a completely illogical perspective, yet making everything suddenly make sense.

Neptune rules the 12th house, the last house in the circular chart wheel - both ending the cycle and leading back into a new one. It is therefore associated with dissolution, the individualized soul returning back into oneness when the physical body deceases. Those who have made near-death experiences know the feeling of being boundless and eternal, at one. Neptune always seeks transcendence and ecstasy. Ecstasy literally means "standing outside" – to leave the body and all other physical restrictions and interpersonal boundaries. Standing outside of yourself can drive you into insanity or madness, but the seduction of letting go of a purely mundane existence is too big for Neptune. This planet gives up reality for ecstasy, making us and our lives heavily unbalanced and unhealthy.

Without the intellectual or pragmatic approach of Uranus, Neptune seeks freedom in different ways: escaping one's self, one's life, and one's mind by reading, writing, or imagining and dreaming of other worlds, watching shows and movies, playing video games or being immersed in other alternative realities, partying and losing oneself either in the crowds or in the dance, alcohol, drugs, and all kinds of substance abuse. Neptune turns into a bad influence when, rather than connecting us to the spiritual realm, it merely disconnects us from reality, it makes us use all kinds of escapism.

This astrological planet is connected to spirituality, mysticism, and the paranormal. At best, it makes us get in touch with the divine, it makes us become a medium or a channel through which God can communicate with the world. Lots of religious messengers and spiritual luminaries are strongly influenced by Neptune. However, so are lots of crazy nut jobs. There's a very thin line between making a transcendental experience and simply going insane, between being declared a Buddha and being sent off to a mental hospital. But both enlightenment and madness are rare and extreme occurrences. The real danger of Neptune is that which every regular "spiritual person" or "positive thinker" faces: spiritual bypassing. This term was coined by John Welwood and refers to spirituality as a defense mechanism or as an avoidance strategy of life and its struggles. By being too positive, too detached, too forgiving, we avoid the reality of tough circumstances, painful feelings, a harsh memory, and the like. Mottos like "Just be positive", "Love thy neighbor", "Look on the bright side", or "Suffering is an illusion created by the ego" can't always be applied. However, both spiritual bypassing and escapism are the specialties of Neptune. Wherever it is placed in our charts, we tend to be in a state of denial. Usually, we avoid the harsh truth by putting on rose-tinted glasses, making this an area of life in which we live in fantasy rather than reality.

Neptune is a dreamer and a poet who sees more meaning in situations than there might actually objectively be. Being caught up in romance, yearnings, melancholy, fantasies, and longings does not have to mean that one is delusional. That which is beyond human understanding, that which eludes scientific explanation, is not always nonsense. Maybe Neptune really has a better hold on reality than other planetary archetypes do – the reality outside of the limits of Newtonian science and the physical world. After all, our solar system is but an atom of the Universe. Neptune teaches us to take "reality" less seriously, to relish in fantasy and dreams and reconnect with the symbolic and subjective experience. Maybe that one is more real after all. Science finds more mysteries each time it makes a discovery. Mystery may be the very nature of reality. Neptune accepts that and loses itself in that.

"I sense the world might be more dreamlike, metaphorical, and poetic than we currently believe—but just as irrational as sympathetic magic when looked at in a typically scientific way. I wouldn't be surprised if poetry—poetry in the broadest sense, in the sense of a world filled with metaphor, rhyme, and recurring patterns, shapes, and designs—is how the world works. The world isn't logical, it's a song."
David Byrne

♆ Neptune in 1st House

Unclear about their role or identity, confusion regarding how they come across (others may see in them whatever they want to see; there is a fog between their real selves and others), naïve and in denial about reality (may be unreliable, gullible, and very sensitive), drift around as passive daydreamers.

♆ Neptune in 2nd House

Unclear about their source of money (but may still blindly trust that they'll always be supported somehow), confusion regarding finances (unpractical and unreliable, may depend on others or has others depend on them), naïve and in denial about the importance of a safe foundation (doesn't see investments or savings as necessary), can be very unclear about what they have to offer or what makes them valuable, which affects their sense of self-worth.

♆ Neptune in 3rd House

Unclear thinking processes (no clear trains of thought), confused mind, may have learning disabilities, naïve and in denial about swindlers and liars (can be tricked easily), a mind that drifts around with vivid daydreams, very imaginative.

♆ Neptune in 4th House

Unclear about their heritage and roots (either literally or through a lack of identification with their family), confusion regarding the parents (especially the mother may have been idealized in the mind of the individual), naïve and in denial about possible mistreatment in childhood (turn the other cheek), drift around without a solid sense of "home", home sickness for a place that exists only in their imagination.

♆ Neptune in 5th House

Unclear about their creative potential (lots of creativity and a vivid imagination that is hard to channel into a piece of art), confusion regarding their own children (if there are any, they will have a hard time understanding them), naïve in romance (rose-tinted glasses), drift around between love affairs, easily seducing others and/or easily being seduced by them.

♆ Neptune in 6th House

Unclear about their duties and responsibilities, confusion regarding their health (illnesses that are hard to diagnose, physically sensitive and weak), naïve about their work (may hold on to the fantasy of an ideal work place and deny that it doesn't exist), drift from one occupation to another (possibly with long periods of unemployment, may work in the spiritual field or help people).

♆ Neptune in 7th House

Unclear about their partners (partners may be deceptive or hard to get a grasp on), naïve and in denial about the reality of their relationships (dream about a soulmate union and will readily sacrifice for their partners, easy to seduce), may drift into relationships as if by fate, high ideals in love, but can be taken advantage of.

♆ Neptune in 8th House

Extreme psychic sensitivity and intuiting of other people's motivations and secrets, may have a fascination with death (interest in life after death, communication with the dead, or even a death wish), trusts others with their money easily and usually lets the partner handle the finances (has to make sure not be swindled by accountants or partners), sex is experienced as a deep union of the souls which can make them either celibate or practice tantric sex.

♆ Neptune in 9th House

Unclear about their worldview and thus can easily turn towards "gurus" (political, religious, or of other kinds) whom they worship and blindly follow, beliefs and philosophy are very mystical or spiritual, high ideals, higher education may be neglected or they may drop out of it, has to learn to turn to their own studies rather than following other people's dogmas.

♆ Neptune in 10th House

Unclear about their career, confusion regarding their vocation and reputation (may be perceived wrongly; as a public figure, they can become a projector screen for collective fantasies – which is good for acting, the entertainment industry, art, and work of service), naïve about their career, may deny that success comes from hard work and thus drift around with little ambition.

♆ Neptune in 11th House

Unclear about their dreams and aspirations (may have

utopian dreams and high ideals which are rather blurry), confusion regarding their future (dreaming about it without making concrete plans), naïve and gullible regarding their friends and other groups of people (gullible towards deceptive friends and liars), may be part of a circle of spiritual or artistic people, friends may introduce them to drugs.

♆ Neptune in 12th House

Unclear about their self-undoing (sacrifice themselves and sabotage themselves unknowingly), very high level of empathy which can result in them doing charity work (usually serve others in unseen ways, "behind the scenes", through secret acts of kindness or in institutions), very forgiving, martyrs, may live in seclusion or even exile, devoted to spiritual or religious practices.

PLUTO

"Perhaps our eyes need to be washed by our tears once in a while, so that we can see life with a clearer view again."
Alex Tan

Pluto is known as the planet of extremes; life and death, power and powerlessness – but more than that, it is about that which is in between the two extremes – that phase of transformation and rebirth. It's about the freedom and relief that comes with letting go – of life, of power, of control, of formerly held ideas about one's life and the self. This is the archetype represented by the phoenix rising out of its own ashes – more beautiful and wise than before.

Pluto represents the primal power of life and death as in renewal and transformation. It indicates either how (Sign) and where (House) we go through powerful changes and are reborn or where we fail to do so and have to go through the same patterns again and again until we recognize them and transform.

To me, Pluto is the planet of surrender and openness, similar to Neptune. Pluto transformations are the most extreme but we can always benefit from them – like a heart being broken so that it can never close itself off again. It is a long path to this surrender, though; it usually starts with a controlling grip, like our life depends on it. And it does, because Pluto will make us die several times in our life – only for us to be reborn as a new, stronger and wiser version of ourselves.

Pluto strips away anything you thought you needed – it leaves you utterly naked and vulnerable – only for you to realize that you really do not need the things you thought you did – it strips away power to make you realize that it was a false idea of control that was in fact controlling you. Like the famous Fight Club quote, "What you own ends up owning you". In Greek mythology, Pluto is associated with Hades, the ruler of the Underworld. When you die, you won't take anything with you into the realm of Hades, such as money, status, respect, influence – all you have is your soul and its wisdom and compassion. Pluto rebirths remind us that the former is not essential and that, in the end, it won't mean anything. The soul is what is essential, because it is immortal.

The paradox of control is that you can only truly be in control if you give it up first. Let me give you an example: Have you ever been in a public place or surrounded by people and trying not to cry? When the tears burn behind your eyes, you are trying to keep them back, control yourself, restrain yourself and somebody goes "Are you okay?" it immediately opens the floodgates. You are embarrassed about crying, you try to hide it, suppress it, but it keeps getting worse. Somebody tells you to stop crying – which makes you cry even harder. If, however, you did not even try to control your tears in the first place, like a little child, who has not yet learned to restrict their emotional expression, you will move through it very quickly. One second, a child will cry and sob and, the next, it will be giggling at a butterfly passing by. If you let go of trying to control something, you will be surprised to see how much more power you will gain. It is really like trying to hold water in a clenched fist and having it seep through your fingers versus holding it in an open palm. It is like struggling to escape from chains, while they are only pulling tighter. It is like swimming against the current, which will only bring you closer to drowning. Let go and let yourself be pulled down the current – surrender to the natural flow and you will regain control. Let go or you will be dragged. Really picture this and see the universal truth in it. You can see this dynamic everywhere – telling someone to stop being shy will actually make them more quiet, telling someone to calm down will make them burn with rage. What you resist, persists. In a storm, the little vulnerable pieces of grass will bend and look the same when the storm has passed. But a tree with deeps roots and a lot of resistance against the storm will break. Pluto rules Scorpio, the fixed water sign – fixed water is kind of like a vortex in the sea. Don't fight it or you will be sucked in.

It is all about giving up the fight, giving up control. Pluto wants you to surrender to making whatever state you are in be completely okay and for you to be present with it unconditionally, not judging it, trying to control it or exert power over it and manipulate it. I once heard that true meditation is not trying to manipulate your experience. Meditation can then not only be a daily practice, but rather a constant state of being – the one which Pluto urges (sometimes even forces) us to reach.

By making everything we think and feel be okay, we will also stop trying to hide it from others. Oftentimes we might feel like keeping secrets, hiding vulnerabilities and not giving everything away will give us more power, more control. Pluto rules secrecy and anything that is being kept in the shadows. Most of all it rules taboos – those things that are absolutely off-limits, not to be mentioned! But Pluto urges us to come to terms with everything, to not manipulate our experience and hence to not keep anything hidden or private. The word privacy comes from the Latin "privo" which means "to deprive", "to rob" or "to strip away", "to lack" or "to be separated from the rest". Privacy is only ever the result of bad experiences, of thinking that if we expose ourselves, we will be judged, used, abused, humiliated, or something along those lines. Pluto makes us fear intrusion and exposure and can therefore make us controlling, manipulative and secretive.

Being Plutonian, intrusion and exposure are my biggest fears. I am terrified of those things. But if I, essentially, fear powerlessness, isn't the greatest act of empowerment to deliberately choose to open up and be utterly vulnerable, to take the power to expose myself so others can't do it, to open up so no one can intrude? You can't break into an open house and you can't strip anything away from a naked person. People can't make fun of you if you laugh and joke about yourself. You have just taken away all their ammunition. It is, however, really hard not to take the parts of the horoscope touched by Pluto super seriously. We try and become bulletproof there, we are controlling and defensive, without realizing that all it takes for us to be bulletproof is to simply take away other people's ammunition. And we do that by letting go of it. Becoming soft, losing resistance. If you shoot a bullet in a plank of wood it will leave a gaping hole. If, however, you were to shoot that bullet into a body of water, no dent will be left. Because there was no resistance against that bullet.

Have you ever heard of the Greek myth of Pandora's Box? Once this box was opened, all bad things were released into the world that had been innocent, pure and happy until this point. Pluto is like Pandora's Box. In it lie hidden and secret all things we feel are bad, wrong, evil and shameful. We fear that exposing any of those unacceptable parts to others, or even just admitting them to ourselves, will open up the box that lets everything bad out at once. But if we do not let it out, it will stay contained within us, torturing us. Opening Pandora's Box is more like a purge, a way of purifying yourself, releasing shame, becoming innocent again.

Digging for your plutonian shadows is like digging for oil – once you hit the source after shoveling away dirt for what feels like forever – it all comes pouring out, seemingly never stopping. It makes you wonder, "All of this was buried so deeply under the ground?" Once you remember an initial trauma, the root, all minor traumas- branches connected to that root – suddenly reconnect and make sense. Then you will realize that cutting off the branches, acting like nothing happened and having a positive attitude won't do. This stuff will just crop up again and again, like weeds. You have to pull out the root.

Keeping things hidden and stored within makes them hurt more. Pluto cracks us open so that light may come in. He rips us out of our cocoon for us to realize we have morphed into something new, our past self does not define us anymore, we now have wings, can let go of what we used to be. We are free and whole and have regained innocence.

The sting of a scorpion is poisonous but the venom can also be used medically for healing. The truth stings, it may hurt – but it will also heal you.

Pluto seems cruel and terrifying. He is utterly ruthless and extreme. But you will thank him later. He is the one who would push you off of the platform if you were about to chicken out of a bungee jump. He is the one who strips off your band-aid so that you can realize the wound has healed and the only reason you kept on holding on to it was you trying to cover it up.

In German, we have a saying along the lines of "You have to jump over your own shadow." This means that this part within or without you that scares you the most, that you fear confronting, will simply go away once you have the courage to face it. This also reminds me of a parable by Tschuang-tse in which a man keeps on running from his own shadow and the sound of his own steps until he dies of exhaustion, without realizing that what makes the shadow disappear is walking into it and what makes the sound of his step fall silent is simply standing still.

Have you ever noticed how everything that is now taboo was once sacred? Pluto wants us to transform taboos back to their sacredness. Sexuality and the naked human body are not "wrong" and therefore should not have to be kept secret about or hidden and covered at all costs – hiding sexuality will make it turn into ugly and destructive forms of it. Remember how everything we think we are controlling is actually controlling us? In the dark, things can take on grotesque forms. Other taboos include death, financial problems, mental illness – but we would all benefit from more open discussions about that, by putting ourselves on the line and being courageous enough to ask for help and support, rather than suffering silently, trying to control and silence ourselves. Stop trying to "Keep it together". If one person can talk about something like their experiences with depression, possibly thousands of people (or even just one person!) can go „Wow, I'm not alone!" This feeling of not being alone in a situation takes you from a place of utter powerlessness and shame to a sense of connection. Overcoming taboos, being open about them, building bridges is truly a form of plutonian empowerment. This openness inspires others.

I want to specify what exactly Plutonian traumas are. Donna Cunningham has written a lot about this in her book "Healing Pluto Problems", which I highly recommend. In this book, she says that Pluto shows where we have felt powerless towards getting something we wanted and have therefore gained a "fail-for-spite" attitude, where we basically subconsciously make ourselves fail again and again in that particular area of life just so that we can tell ourselves "It wasn't in my control, I am wired for failure when it comes to this!"

We end up telling ourselves "Whatever, who really needs

that anyway, right?" But only someone who really suffered by not getting that thing they really wanted would say that. "I don't really need that, I'm above stuff like that – it doesn't really control me." But it does, because you are pulling into the opposite direction of "pseudo-independence" of it. Pretending not to need or want that thing is just a defense mechanism of powerlessness. When we go to the other extreme of what has been withheld from us, then it still controls us, because our actions are still reactions to that. For example: someone with Pluto in the 11th house might have felt powerless towards belonging to a group of friends and fitting in and therefore develops an attitude of "Whatever, I don't need anyone, I will just be by myself from now on!" (that was me by the way) Do you see how going to the other extreme shows that it still controls us?

The biggest thing we have to learn through Pluto is admitting our dependency on something, needing something, being controlled by something or someone and that thing or person or group of people having power over us. The ultimate form of vulnerability is admitting something has power over you. Abuse victims often tell themselves they deserve their abuse or that they have caused it, because that leaves them a sense of control over the situation. But reaching the point of vulnerability where you absolutely admit and surrender to your powerlessness and being controlled in that area of life is what will free you. Hanging onto it is more torture than letting go.

Pluto in the houses shows where we feel threatened because of an initial (minor or major) trauma of being powerless. We keep on expecting invasion and tyranny by others in this area of life. This is why we can become paranoid, obsess over it. To avoid the powerlessness we expect or feel we are in, we can become controlling, manipulative, secretive and seek other ways of gaining power in devious ways. It shows the very darkest parts of what people are capable of.

It also shows where we tear down everything we have build just to renew it. To quote Donnie Darko, "Destruction is a form of creation". You have to tear down and destroy something to rebuild it and make something better blossom from these fertile grounds. Pluto is actually exalted in the sign of Leo. Leo is the expressive and artistic creator so it makes sense that this energy greatly supports Pluto's tendency towards destruction – to create something new. I am Plutonian, meaning Pluto is the dominant planet in my chart and I am generally a really destructive person – I rip apart pages from old diaries so that no one can ever read them, impulsively delete social media accounts and have gone from light blonde to dark brown hair just because I was aching for a transformation. The house Pluto is in thus also indicates in which area of our lives we will go through a lot of these destruction-creation processes, destroying the old and tearing it down to make place for a new beginning, a fresh start.

♇ Pluto in 1st House

Has felt powerless regarding how they are perceived by others, which now makes them paranoid about losing control over that. Can be secretive about who they are, because there is shame attached to it. Will experience many transformations and rebirths in their personality and self-presentation. Fear that self and persona is controlled or manipulated, under threat by others, paranoid about losing power over who they are and therefore completely reinvents themselves again and again.

♇ Pluto in 2nd House

Has felt powerless regarding personal and financial resources which now makes them paranoid about losing control over that. Denies needing money. Can be secretive about their finances, because there is shame attached to this topic. Will experience many transformations and rebirths in what they value. This fits the idea of "What you own ends up owning you." We think things give us power but they have power over us. Can go from greed and saving to uncontrolled spending.

♇ Pluto in 3rd House

Has felt powerless regarding the sharing of their thoughts and opinions which now makes them paranoid about losing control over that. Can be inhibited about speaking up, because there is shame attached to their knowledge or lack thereof. Feel they're powerless about expressing their thoughts and opinions, like they are not heard, their intellect is belittled, their message not received or their words twisted in their mouths. Will have to reach a point of feeling so utterly out of control of their self-expression that it makes them want to scream and write their thoughts in bold red letters on all the walls. They will be heard, become powerful communicators with a magnetic way of speaking that transforms others opinions.

♇ Pluto in 4th House

Has felt powerless at home and in their family which now makes them paranoid about losing control in this area. Can be secretive about their past, because there is shame attached to it. Not only regarding their family but also where they're coming from in terms of development of their very soul and inner self. Will experience many transformations and rebirths in their relationship with their roots and heritage.

♇ Pluto in 5th House

Has felt powerless regarding the giving and receiving of love which now makes them paranoid about losing control over that. Denies needing love and will turn it into a game of power. Can be a seductive flirt. Can be secretive about their true passions, because there is shame attached to it. Will experience many transformations and rebirths in their recreational activities and romantic flings.

♇ Pluto in 6th House

Has felt powerless regarding the fulfillment of their tasks and work in general which now makes them paranoid about losing control over that and, consequently, turns them into a workaholic. Denies needing to be needed. Will experience many transformations and rebirths in their health and can be a powerful healer. Will obsess over work-related projects and be secretive about them. Might feel that their co-workers are always out to get them.

♇ Pluto in 7th House

Has felt powerless regarding the building of healthy relationships which now makes them paranoid about losing control over that. Denies needing relationships ("I'm fine on my own"). Can be secretive with others but still want to know all of *their* secrets. Will experience many transformations and rebirths in how they relate to others. Power games in relationships.

♇ Pluto in 8th House

Has felt powerless regarding their own psychological and sexual drives which now makes them paranoid about losing control over that. Obsessed with taboos and control – hypnotic and powerful effect and influence on others, might abuse their power. Will experience many transformations and rebirths through intimacy (sexual and personal).

♇ Pluto in 9th House

Has felt powerless to God or the universe, thinking there is a higher power out to get them, which now makes them paranoid about losing control over that. Either denies needing a religion or ideology or is obsessed with one. Will experience many transformations and rebirths in their ideologies, worldview and philosophy of life. Extreme views (atheism, theism...).

♇ Pluto in 10th House

Has felt powerless regarding their public image and choice of career which now makes them paranoid about losing control over that. Denies needing success but really wants to have power and impact. Might want to deal with secrets and research in their career. Will experience many transformations in their reputation and life goals.

♇ Pluto in 11th House

Denies needing a network of supportive people. Has felt powerless to find belonging in a group of people, friendship circles have constantly shifted, old friendships seem to end and new ones to begin all the time, never truly finds a place they fit into, feel they can't ever open up because the friends are never quite the right ones, friendship are never really deep and meaningful because they're guarded and secretive. By opening up, they can create powerful bonds.

♇ Pluto in 12th House

Feels like their own subconscious mind is constantly out to get them. They are their own worst enemy and can't trust themselves. Can go through powerful transformations by isolating themselves and being with themselves for a period of time, learning to trust their own mind. Might be psychic but tell themselves they are imagining things, that their mind is tricking them. Natural healer.

EPILOGUE

Authenticity can become a mask. If you find out who you are and decide to authentically present this to the world, it can turn into a character you're playing. A carved-out identity is never authentic.

You might not be who you are now in two years time. You might not be who you are now in two seconds time. Who you are is constantly changing, it is not a set personality, it is fluid like water, it can change and mold all the time and flow everywhere.

Authenticity means becoming okay with not knowing who you are. Authenticity is not finding yourself or creating yourself, it is simply being yourself.

Being means not doing.

Authenticity is not a job, there is no effort in it, you don't have to find yourself and add those traits of your real self. You just have to subtract inauthenticity, you have to subtract the fears that restrict your self-expression, make you tell white lies, make you feel like you have to be something else, fake it 'till you make it.

Authenticity is not about addition, it's about subtraction. Authenticity is effortless. It's not trying.

As soon as you know "who you are", you can fall into the trap of playing a role. The key to being yourself is *allowing*. Non-resistance. Letting who you are flow through you and into the world without any expectations or rules of what that will look like.

Surprise yourself. Shake the core of your self-concept. If who you are was water, your self-image would be a container. It gives structure and definition but it also limits you.

Living authentically is being art, not the artist. You let the divine take over and the celestial paint brush will paint you across the cosmos. Surrender to being painted, instead of being the painter. You are a creation of the universe, so let it flow through you in order to become the masterpiece you were meant to be.

Made in the USA
San Bernardino, CA
14 August 2016